William Lackland

Meteors, aërolites, storms, and atmospheric phenomena

William Lackland

Meteors, aërolites, storms, and atmospheric phenomena

ISBN/EAN: 9783337716974

Printed in Europe, USA, Canada, Australia, Japan

Cover: Foto ©ninafisch / pixelio.de

More available books at **www.hansebooks.com**

METEORS,

AËROLITES, STORMS, AND ATMOSPHERIC PHENOMENA.

FROM THE FRENCH OF

ZÜRCHER AND MARGOLLÉ.

BY

WILLIAM LACKLAND.

ILLUSTRATED WITH TWENTY-THREE FINE WOODCUTS, BY LEBRETON.

NEW YORK:
D. APPLETON AND COMPANY,
90, 92 & 94 GRAND STREET.
1870.

ENTERED, according to act of Congress, in the year 1869, by
D. APPLETON & CO.,
in the Clerk's Office of the District Court of the United States for the Southern District of New York.

PREFACE.

The nations of antiquity contemplated the grand spectacles that Nature offers with emotions different from ours. Their admiration partook more largely of amazement and fear.

We read in the *Vedas*, or sacred books of India, the following sentences:

"Will the sun rise again?

"Will our beloved aurora return?

"Will the powers of the night be conquered by the god of day?"

To us these questions seem strange. Were they put in earnest? Were the men of the earliest ages serious when they asked themselves anxiously at night whether the light of day would overcome the darkness, and reappear at dawn to restore sunshine, heat, and life, to the world?

Yes, there is no doubt of it; history attests the fact; the earliest nations thought that the stars were animated, living bodies. In their eyes the heavenly bodies were superior beings, good or bad deities, friends or enemies, and ever ready to engage in conflicts of which the issue might be favorable or injurious to mortals.

The Aurora, or Dawn, itself was one of these divinities, and the most charming of them. Always beautiful with freshness and youth, she was ever saluted and hailed with gratitude, because she it was who came the first to announce the defeat of the powers of darkness and evil, and each morning, like a tender and faithful messenger, awoke the sons of men.

It is not with these childlike feelings that we moderns contemplate the sublime scenery of creation. We never entertain a doubt in our day of the regular reappearance of the sun; we know beforehand the hour, the minute, nay, the very second of his rising, and we can calculate with precision the length of the dawn in different climes. But this happy certainty, which we owe to science and experience, has not weakened the sense of admiration in our souls. On the contrary, this religious and prolific feeling has increased in strength, in elevation, and has become more and more chastened as reflection and study have gradually revealed to us, with greater force of testimony, the infinite power and goodness of the Great Being who presides over the universe. We follow with an interest full of poetic thought the progress of the human mind in the study of these natural forces, these material agents, these vast springs of life and motion, that obey the will of God, and of which the ancients had only so confused an idea. How vast a field is here opened to observation, even when limited to the phenomena which have merely the terrestrial atmosphere for their theatre! What a variety of effects are produced around us by the action, and by the incessant combinations, of the three elements — air, fire, and water *— which serve to maintain and develop life in all its grades and in all its forms on the surface of the globe!

It has been said with truth by Ernest Faivre,

* Atmospheric phenomena are usually divided into aërial, aqueous, or igneous meteors.

in his book entitled "The Scientific Works of Goethe:" "The spectacle of the various conditions of the sky; the changing aspects of the clouds, the rain, the hail, and the tempest, as they form above our heads; the appearance of luminous meteors, such as the aurora borealis, the halo, and the rainbow, have in them something marvellous that enchains attention; and for an intelligence capable of deep appreciation such studies must have a resistless charm."

CONTENTS.

CHAPTER I.

THE ILLUMINATION OF THE ATMOSPHERE.—TWILIGHT.—THE MIRAGE.

The Atmosphere.—The Azure Vault of the Sky.—The Prolongation of Daylight.—Colors of the Spectrum.—Twilight in the Polar Regions.—The Anti-Twilight.—The Mirage.—The Fata Morgana............ 13

CHAPTER II.

CLOUDS AND FOGS.

The Clouds.—Formation of the Clouds and Mists.—Influence of the Marine Currents.—Extraordinary Fogs.—Appearance and Motion of the Clouds.—Hail-Clouds.—Forms of the Clouds.—Cloud-Rings.—Influence of the Mountains.—Distribution of the Clouds.—The Spectre of the Brocken.—The Shadow of Mont Blanc....................... 34

CHAPTER III.

RAIN, SNOW, AND HAIL.

Dew.—White Frost.—The Distribution of Rain on the Surface of the Globe.—The Great Rains of India.—Regions without Rain.—Influence of Forests.—The Softening of Climates.—Forms of the Snow.—Flowers under the Snow.—Glaciers and Rivers.—Hail.............61

CHAPTER IV.

PHENOMENA OF THE GLACIERS.

Meteorology of the Glaciers.—Their Formation.—The Grindelwald and Furca Glaciers. — Amphitheatres.—Névés.—Moraines.—Movements of the Glaciers.—Primitive Glaciers.—Polar Glaciers.—Variations of the Seasons and Climate.. 86

CHAPTER V.

THUNDER-STORMS.

Luminous Phenomena.—The Fires of St. Elmo.—Thunder-storms among the Mountains.—The Forms of Lightning.—Globular Thunder-bolts.— Thunder.—Singular Effects of Lightning.—Lightning-rods.—Geography of Thunder-storms.—Influence of the Soil.—Volcanic Storms.— Action of Thunder-storms upon the Subterranean Waters.—Utility of Thunder-storms.. 104

CHAPTER VI.

WHIRLWINDS.

Water-spouts.—Electric Whirlwinds.—Sand-storms.—Water-spouts at Sea. — Water-spouts on Land. — Tornadoes. — Cyclones. — Hurricanes.. 139

CHAPTER VII.

RAINBOWS.—CROWNS, AND HALOS.

Description of the Rainbow.—Play of Light in the Drops of Water.— Varied Appearances of the Arch.—Supplementary Arcs.—The Circles of Ulloa.—Crowns.—Colored Arcs.—Parhelia.—White Arcs.— Anthelia.—The Halo of Cléré...................................... 170

CONTENTS. 9

CHAPTER VIII.

THE AURORAL LIGHTS.

General Description.—Icy Fog.—Noise and Odor.—Electrical Currents.—Magnetic Influence.—The Aurora Australis.—Different Points of View.—Periodicity of the Auroral Lights. 190

CHAPTER IX.

SHOOTING-STARS.

Fire-balls.—Showers of Stones.—Meteoric Stones.—An Extraordinary Meteor.—Velocity and Appearance of Fire-balls.—The Fall of Aërolites.—Periodical Reappearances.—Composition of Aërolites.—Darkening of the Sun.—Ring of Meteorites......................... 207

CHAPTER X.

DUST IN THE ATMOSPHERE.—DRY FOGS.

Cosmic Dust.—Volcanic Ashes.—The Sands of the Deserts.—The Red Mists of Cape Verde.—Showers of Manure.—Dry Fogs.......... 235

CHAPTER XI.

PROGNOSTICS OF THE WEATHER.

Progress of Meteorology. — Foretelling the Weather. — Orpheus, Homer, Hesiod, Virgil.—Prognostics furnished by Animals.—Prognostics from Plants, and from the State of the Sky.—Characters of the Seasons and of Future Years.—Shooting-Stars.—Influence of the Moon.. 261

CHAPTER XII.

PRACTICAL METEOROLOGY.

The Brussels Conference.—Meteorological Practice.—Instruments of Observation.—Telegraphic Meteorology.—The Hurricane of December 2, 1863.—Alarm-Signals.—Rural Meteorology.—Association for the Advancement of Meteorology................................. 286

NOTES.

INSTRUMENTS OF OBSERVATION.

The Barometer.—The Thermometer.—The Hygrometer.—The Pluviometer or Udometer.......... 319

LIST OF ILLUSTRATIONS.

	PAGE
THE MIRAGE,	25
FATA MORGANA,	30
CIRRUS AND STRATUS,	48
NIMBUS AND CUMULUS,	49
SPECTRE OF THE BROCKEN,	55
SHAPES OF SNOW-FLAKES,	77
THE LYSE-FIORD,	131
A VOLCANIC STORM,	133
A WATER-SPOUT,	148
A HURRICANE,	163
A RAINBOW,	170
WATERFALL RAINBOWS,	173
THE CIRCLE OF ULLOA,	178
HALOS,	182
THE AURORA BOREALIS,	190
THE HURWORTH METEOR,	214
SHOWER OF SHOOTING-STARS,	227
A WILL-O'-THE-WISP,	255
THE STORM-GLASS,	294
ALARM-SIGNALS,	306
THE PLUVIOMETER,	323

METEORS AND METEORIC PHENOMENA.

CHAPTER I.

*THE ILLUMINATION OF THE ATMOSPHERE.—
TWILIGHT.—THE MIRAGE.*

The Atmosphere.—The Azure Vault of the Sky.—The Prolongation of Daylight.—Colors of the Spectrum.—Twilight in the Polar Regions.—The Anti-Twilight.—The Mirage.—The Fata Morgana.

THE ATMOSPHERE.

" THE atmosphere surrounds the earth with a spherical envelope, or wrapping, the thickness of which is unknown.[1]

"However, numerous observations have indicated that the limit of this atmospheric envelope cannot be either less or more than a little over sixty-two miles.

"This atmosphere, although invisible, presses on the surface of our bodies at the rate of fifteen

[1] It will always be impossible, perhaps, to attain a rigorously accurate estimate, because the rarefaction of the upper layers augments precisely as the height is greater and the pressure less.

pounds per square inch, so that each of us carries about, without feeling it, a total weight of nearly 35,000 pounds.

"Lighter than the lightest down, less palpable than the most delicate filaments, it leaves intact the spider's web, and hardly bends upon their stalks the flowers that it refreshes with its dews; yet it bears with it around the world the ships of all nations on its wings, and crushes the hardest rock or metal with its weight. When in motion, it is strong enough to uproot the loftiest trees, and overturn the most substantial monuments, to toss the ocean in furious billows, and shatter the proudest vessels as though they were but toys.

"The atmosphere heats and cools, by turns, the earth and all the creatures that inhabit it.

"It drinks up the mists which it holds aloft in overarching clouds, and then showers them down in rain or dew upon the thirsty ground.

"It refracts and reflects the rays of the sun, in order that it may give us dawn and twilight, and make the heavens glow with dazzling colors when the great luminary rises and sets.

"Were it not for the atmosphere, the sun would come to us and leave us abruptly, and we should pass without transition from the gloom of midnight to the blaze of noon. We should no longer enjoy the soft radiance of twilight, nor would the clouds any longer shade the earth to protect it from the burning heat of the day.

"The atmosphere brings us the elements that sustain the flame of life, as they do the fire on the hearth; and it receives and transmutes in its breast all the deleterious substances thrown off by decomposition. By its circulation it brings us all together in a common life of interchange and mutual dependence. A gaseous substance which would be fatal to us, to wit, the carbonic acid which we constantly inhale and throw off, it disperses over every part of the globe.

"The date-palms of the Nile, the cedars of Lebanon, the cocoa-nut-trees of Tahiti, imbibe it to improve their growth, and the palms and banana-trees of Japan transform its poisonous breath to flowers. That healthful substance, the oxygen which we breathe, comes from the magnolias of the Susquehanna; the splendid trees that fringe the Amazon and Orinoco; the giant rhododendrons of the Himalayas; the roses and the myrtles of Cashmere; the cinnamon-trees of Ceylon, and the ancient forests that stud the interior of Africa. All contribute to supply the agent of life."[1]

[1] See Dr. Buist, in the *Transactions of the Bombay Geographical Society*, vol. ix., 1850.

THE AZURE VAULT OF THE SKY.—THE PROLONGATION OF DAYLIGHT.

The uppermost regions of the atmosphere are not illuminated by daylight. They are given over to eternal night. At a certain height, we begin to see the diffused radiance produced by the particles of the air acting on the rays of the sun, like the thousand facets of a crystal, gradually die out. To the eyes of aëronauts at the height of eight or ten thousand feet above the earth's surface, the stars seem to be shining through the deepest night, while beneath them the earth is glowing with the sun. The beautiful blue tint that appears to us to belong to the sky itself is really only that of the air beheld in masses. It grows darker above the luminous region that immediately surrounds us.

The vault that we seem to gaze upon does not exist. The atmospheric layers, augmenting in density as they approach the terrestrial surface, lend this deceptive appearance to the sky. It took a long time to overcome this illusion, and to establish the fact that the form and the dimensions of the celestial vault change with the condition of the atmosphere, its opaqueness or transparency, and its greater or less degree of illumination.

The rays of the sun are partly extinguished in the air through which they pass. Their diminution is much less at the zenith than at the horizon, where they have to traverse a layer of the atmosphere fifteen times as thick. Thus we can fix our gaze upon the great luminary without being dazzled when it has just risen. A modification of the same nature takes place in terrestrial objects which are less and less easily seen as their distance augments—"'tis distance" "robes the mountain in its azure hue."

This tint so peculiar to the atmosphere is frequently altered by the watery particles which it contains, and which generally throw off white light; this serves to explain the variations observable in the sky where the blue is more decided at the zenith than at the horizon. The color of the same part of the sky often changes in the course of the day. It grows deeper and deeper as we advance from morning until noon, and then insensibly fades until evening.

A very simple experiment will assist us in comprehending that property of light which is called refraction. Put a penny on the bottom of a wide empty vase, or basin, and step back until the coin is hidden from your view; then, without changing your position again, you will see the penny come into view whenever some water is poured into the basin. This is because the light follows a broken line, and the same thing happens whenever it has to pass from a volume of air of greater to one of less density. In like manner may we explain that other phenomenon of the atmosphere which, by refracting the rays of the sun, causes us to see it at a greater elevation than the real one, and thus perceptibly increases the length of the day.

Before rising, the sun illuminates the higher ranges of cloud, and they reflect his light to us. This light gradually increases until his disk appears. The directly opposite effect takes place in the evening, when the sun is setting. Who has not often admired those successive transitions, those struggles between day and night, that offer so sublime a spectacle, endlessly varied by the thousand colors of the vapors spread along the horizon, and the clouds that float in the sky?

THE COLORS OF THE SOLAR SPECTRUM.

If we cause the solar light to pass through a prism of crystal, it produces a colored spectrum. This spreading forth of different hues, which has an almost magical effect, is produced by the decomposition of a white ray into several kinds of

THE COLORS OF THE SOLAR SPECTRUM. 19

light, of which the seven principal hues follow each other in the subjoined order :

Violet, indigo, blue, green, yellow, orange, red.

That property of the atmosphere which produces this phenomenon is designated in science by the name of dispersion.

Mr. Forbes, an English physiologist, has made and described a very curious observation of the play of light in vapors suspended in the air. This observation assists us in comprehending the phenomena visible during the morning and evening twilight.

Mr. Forbes was standing near a locomotive that was about to start, and was looking at the image of the sun reflected in the column of steam that issued from the 'scape-pipe.

Immediately over the orifice, the vapor was clear and transparent like the air. The sun's rays passed it without diminution of strength, and fell upon a white wall opposite. A little higher up, the light appeared less vivid, but the color was orange, and the half shade thrown upon the wall reminded the observer of the first tints of evening. The disk of the sun just above it was of a deep-red color. Beyond that the steam, before resolving itself into drops of water, would not allow the rays to pass, and its shadow was completely dark.

SUNSET.

On the Atlantic Ocean, near the coast of Portugal, we have noticed twilight in which the colors of the spectrum succeeded each other with great regularity, from bluish green to vivid red. These modifications are slow in our climate; they permit us to enjoy fully the magic spectacle of those twilight scenes in which the sombre blue of the sea heightens the delicate hues of the sky. Near the equator, the duration of the phenomenon is much less, but it is generally extremely beautiful. M. Liais, a French astronomer of eminence, has thus described it in the narrative of his voyage to Rio Janeiro:

"Almost immediately after the setting of the sun, a rosy tinge is seen in the east. Then there soon becomes visible above it a dark segment of sky, frequently of a greenish color. The rosy hue extends and broadens toward north and south, and, eleven minutes after its appearance in the east, begins to be seen in the west, the zenith remaining blue. In reality, a rosy coloring exists all around the zenith, clear to the horizon, excepting at the east, where a grayish blue or greenish gray rests on the horizon, and at the west, where a white

SUNSET. 21

segment may be noticed. Eight minutes after its appearance in the west, the rosy coloring which had remained all the time at the west, but was gradually growing feebler, disappears altogether on that side. At the west can be distinguished a white segment, bordered with an arc of vivid rose-color, above which appears the deep azure with a splendor and intensity of tint impossible to describe. This arc descends, gradually, toward the horizon. It then becomes greatly flattened and assumes a vivid scarlet or orange red. It sets, at length, when the sun is 11° below the horizon.

"When the red arc is very low, and on the point of disappearing at the west, a second rosy coloring appears gradually and simultaneously at the west and the east, making a complete circuit of the zenith, which remains blue all the time. At the west, a space of silvery white separates the two rose-colored arcs. By degrees, as the sun descends, the second rosy coloring is seen to disappear first at the east, withdrawing toward the north and south without passing by the zenith. Then, at last, the first rose-colored arc sets, and there remains only the second arc, which is in the west, and has the form of a flattened arch, with a white segment below it. Finally, this second rose-colored arc, which assumes a still redder hue as it descends, sets when the sun is 18° below the horizon."

We will also quote the description of a sunset on the Desert of Sahara, as given by M. Charles Martins in the *Revue des Deux Mondes*, August 15, 1864:

"Each sunset was a veritable feast for our eyes, and a delight as well as a source of astonishment for the mind, especially when the atmosphere was not completely serene. The coloring of the sky is then more vivid and more varied. Gradually, as the sun approaches the horizon, the gray dishevelled clouds of the overarching sky—those latest emissaries of the northern mists and fogs—become fringed with purple tints that grow more and more intense, while the rounded contours of the white clouds reposing on the distant summits take on a yellow bordering, and seem to be set and chased in the rich gold that fills the western heavens. So soon as the sun has descended below the horizon, the softest ruddy tint spreads over the whole western sky. An emanation of the departed luminary, it colors all the mountains. One of these, visible from Biskra, is called *Djebel-Hammar-Kreddou*—the mountain with the rosy cheek. It deserves this name, because, long after the setting of the sun, it retains a rosy hue, like the blush of a young girl. Through the effect of contrast with the red, the blue of the sky assumes a watery-green tinge. Little by little the rose-color fades, the illuminated arc contracts, and the light that shines on it is as white and pure as that which should glow in the realms of space beyond the limits of our atmosphere. Thanks to the transparency of the atmosphere, all the outlines of terrestrial objects are clearly defined. The delicate edges of the leaves of the palm-tree become more visible than in the full light of day, and when the whole tree stands out against these backgrounds of alternate yellow, red, and white, it seems as though the poetic beauty of this noble plant were revealed, for the first time, to the gaze. However, night comes on. The planets and then the grand constellations first appear; the sky becomes peopled with myriads of stars. The upper vault grows brighter, and the milky way, which is but a dim, whitish belt, as seen in the higher latitudes, looks like a sparkling scarf of diamonds flung athwart the celestial dome. The moon is no longer that pallid star whose melancholy glance seems to sympathize with the dulness of our foggy regions; it is a glowing disk of the purest silver, that reflects without weakening the rays that it receives, or is a crescent rounded off to the full orb, by the ashy radiance which distinctly and sharply defines the entire outline. Such was the sunset of December 13, 1863, on the evening before our departure from Biskra; it affected us deeply, for it was our adieu to our evenings on the desert."

THE TWILIGHT OF THE POLAR REGIONS.—THE ANTI-TWILIGHT.

The rule generally admitted for the duration of the twilight is the descent of the sun 18° below the horizon. In many places, however, it lasts all night, at certain periods of the year.* In the Scandinavian countries, in northern Germany, and even as low down as the latitude of Paris, this is the case about the period of the summer solstice.

When the upper regions of the atmosphere are filled with fine particles of ice, the darkness is not complete even when the sun is 30° below the horizon, as the long twilights of the polar regions sufficiently prove. In those gloomy countries there reigns, during the six months' night, a sort of half daylight, which is sometimes strong enough to read by, should the effulgence of the moon and the radiance of the *aurora borealis* aid the pale emanations of the sun.

THE MIRAGE.

Very frequently one may notice, after the setting of the sun, when one is standing on an eminence, a red arch defined upon the eastern sky around a darkish-blue space. Under favorable circumstances, the line of separation is marked by a yellowish edging. This is the phenomenon that has been styled the *anti-twilight*. The apex, or culminating point of the arch, is directly opposite the sun, and attentive examination shows that the segment illuminated only by the scattered rays corresponds with the shadow of the earth projected against the sky.

THE MIRAGE.

If in summer we look at objects visible across a field heated by the sun, they seem to waver and their shapes continually change. This effect is accounted for by the crossing and recrossing of thin streams of cold and warm air rising and descending. The luminous rays in passing through them modify their movements at nearly every instant.

The phenomenon known as the *mirage*, of which the most remarkable examples are met with in Egypt, have an analogous origin. In that country the atmosphere is usually calm and extremely pure. At sunrise remote objects can be seen with the most perfect distinctness. From the borders of the Nile to the limits of the Desert, arise, from point to point, small eminences crowned with villages and groves of palm-trees, which look down upon each year's inundation of the river. Gradually, as the sun climbs above the horizon, the ground, becoming heated, imparts its superior temperature to the lower strata of the atmosphere. At such times, the undulating, tremulous motion of which we have spoken is frequently noticed. But when there is no wind, and the dead calm of the atmosphere allows the lower strata to expand without commingling with those that are resting upon them, the spectator might fancy that he had before him a huge lake, in the midst of which are seen the reversed images of the surrounding eminences and the villages that are built upon them. The magnificent blue sky seems to be reflected in it too; but, as one approaches, the imaginary sheet of water fades away, leaving only the burning sands in its place, while farther on the same deceptive picture is reproduced under a different aspect.

These appearances often misled the French troops in Egypt. Worn out with forced marches, dying of thirst under the scorching heat of an African sun, and choked by the clouds of sand that filled the air, they would rush headlong toward the fancied water before them, but the delusive shore, alas! always fled farther and farther at their approach.

To the distinguished *savant* Monge, who accompanied the French expedition into Egypt, is due the elucidation of this phenomenon. He has demonstrated that the most rarefied strata of air, in this case, being the lowermost, a luminous ray darting from an elevated object toward the ground, deflects more and more in consequence of refraction, up to the moment when it is reflected from a last stratum, as it would be from a mirror, and then rises again, subject to a series of refractions the reverse of those first encountered. It thus at last strikes the eye of the observer in the same direction as though it came from a point situated below the level of the soil, presenting the reversed images as they would appear if he saw them on the surface of a placid lake.

Mariners frequently get a view of the *mirage* under circumstances the opposite of those that we have just set forth. The temperature of the sea, being colder than that of the superincumbent strata of air, renders them less dense below than above, and the reversed picture of distant shores or vessels is defined on the atmosphere itself.

Captain Scoresby made many such observations in the waters of Greenland.

"On the 19th of June, 1822," says this accomplished navigator, in one of his narratives, "the sun was very warm, and the coast seemed suddenly to come from fifteen to twenty miles nearer. The highlands were raised so much to the view that we could see them as well from the deck of the ship as we could previously from the foretop. The ice on the horizon assumed the most singular forms; huge blocks looked like pillars and columns; the icebergs and field-ice resembled a chain of prismatic rocks, and at many points the ice appeared to be in the air at a considerable height above the horizon. The ships that happened to be near us had the most fantastic aspect. On some of them the mainsail seemed to be reduced to a mere nothing, while the foresail looked several times as large as it really is.

"Above the vessels at a distance, we saw an exact picture of themselves, but reversed and magnified. In some cases this was at quite an elevation above the ship, but then it was always smaller than the original. For some minutes we saw the image of a vessel that was really below the horizon, and one ship was surmounted by a picture of two like it, the one upright and the other reversed."

Among the numerous varieties of this phenomenon of the *mirage*, the one observed by Messrs. Soret and Jurine on the Lake of Geneva, which might be correctly styled the *lateral* or *horizontal* mirage, is not the least curious. These gentlemen were at a window in the second story of a house close to the shore, and were looking with a spy-glass at a number of sail-boats passing from right to left, in the middle of the lake, while, nearer to the shore, the same fleet of boats appeared to be sailing in exactly the opposite direction! This was an illusion analogous to the Egyptian mirage, and explicable in the same way. Close to the shore the air had been in the shade a part of the morning, and was comparatively cooler, while out in the open lake it had been heated by the blaze of the sun. Hence, *vertical* strata of air of different densities had remained motionless, or nearly so, in the prevailing calm, and refraction had produced its magical effects from side to side, instead of above and below, as in the cases previously detailed.

When, instead of occurring in level and regular strata, these effects of refraction and reflection take place in curved and irregular strata, a mirage is produced in which the images are distorted in every respect, broken or repeated over and over again, and separated for considerable distances from each other. This is what takes place in the fantastic aërial vision formerly ascribed to the fairy *Fata Morgana*, and sometimes attracts multitudes to the sea-shore at Naples, and at Reggio on the Sicilian coast.

"For an extent of several miles along the coast of Sicily," says an eye-witness of this extraordinary spectacle, "I saw the sea assume the appearance of a chain of gloomy mountains, while the waters in the direction of Calabria remained perfectly smooth. Above them was seen, in *chiaro-oscuro*, a range of many thousand pillars, all of equal height, distance, and degrees of light and shade. In the twinkling of an eye, these pilasters lost half their height, and seemed to bend over and resolve themselves into arches and arcades like the old Roman aqueducts. Then a cornice formed along the top, and an endless number of castles, all alike, appeared. These presently faded away into towers that vanished also, leaving nothing visible but a long colonnade, succeeded in its turn by windows, and then by pines and cypresses also indefinitely repeated."

Sometimes these objects are depicted in the sky at a great height above the ground. On such occasions some of them are in rapid motion, while

FATA MORGANA.

others are at rest. Their outlines often gleam with rainbow colors, and, as the light augments, their form becomes more and more aërial, until they melt away and disappear when the sun shines forth in all his splendor.

Bernardin de Saint Pierre relates the following incidents: "A very singular phenomenon was once described to me by our celebrated painter, Vernet, who was my friend. During his youth, when in Italy, he devoted himself particularly to the study of the sky, a more interesting branch of his art, no doubt, than the study of the antique, since it is from the sources of light that the colors and aërial perspectives issue that form the charm of pictures as well as of Nature itself. Vernet, in order to fix their variations, had conceived the idea of painting on the leaves of a book all the shadings of each principal color, and then had marked them with different numbers. When he was designing a sky, after having sketched out his rough draft and the forms of the clouds, he would rapidly note down all the fugitive tints on his canvas with figures corresponding to those in his book, and then color them at his leisure. One day he was greatly astonished to see in the sky the appearance of a city reversed. He could perfectly distinguish the steeples, the towers, and the houses. He hurriedly made a sketch of the phenomenon, and then, determined to know the cause of it, he set out, following the direction of the wind, into the mountains. But what was his surprise when, some twenty miles distant, he found the very city the spectre of which he had beheld in the sky, and had a sketch of in his portfolio!"

It is perhaps to the effects of mirage that we must attribute the extraordinary faculty of sight once so famous on the *Ile de France*. Toward the close of the last century, a colonist named Bottineau could make out vessels which were still a considerable distance below the horizon. The new science which he pretended to have constructed, by combining the effects produced by distant objects upon the water and upon the atmosphere, he called *Nauscopy*. He went to Paris, provided with letters from the intendant and the governor of the island, attesting the reality of his discovery; but he could not even succeed in obtaining an audience with M. de Castries, who was then Minister of Marine. No one took the pains to investigate the means by which he mastered such surprising results. In the latter, Arago was not altogether an unbeliever, as we glean from his efforts to discover whether certain phenomena of the twilight, in which the shadows of distant mountains probably play a part, would not help to clear up this important secret. The poor colonist returned to his home on the Isle of France, where he was afterward seen passing most of his time, until he died, on the sea-shore, his gaze fixed on the horizon, and continuing to excite the amazement of all by the accuracy of his predictions.

CHAPTER II.

CLOUDS AND FOGS.

The Clouds.—Formation of the Clouds and Mists.—Influence of the Marine Currents.—Extraordinary Fogs.—Appearance and Motion of the Clouds.—Hail-Clouds.—Forms of the Clouds.—Cloud-Rings.—Influence of the Mountains.—Distribution of the Clouds.—The Spectre of the Brocken.—The Shadow of Mont Blanc.

THE CLOUDS.

ARISTOPHANES, in his play of *The Clouds*, puts the following invocation into the mouth of Socrates:

" ' O sovereign master! thou vast air that dost envelop all parts of the earth!—luminous ether! and ye, O venerable goddesses, the clouds, mothers of the thunder and the lightning!—arise, O sovereign clouds! and appear on the empyrean heights. Come, O august clouds! whether ye rest on the sacred summits of Olympus, white with snow; or, in the plains of the Ocean, your father, ye form dances in honor of the nymphs; whether at the mouths of the Nile ye dip up his waters in golden urns, or whether ye dwell on the Palus Mæotis, or upon the stormy rock of Mimas, hearken to my prayers, and receive with favor the sacrifice I make.'

"*Chorus of Clouds.*—'Eternal clouds, from the resounding bed of the Ocean, our father, let us rise, in light, transparent mists, to the woody summits of the lofty mountains, that we may look down into the distance upon the hilly country; the sacred earth, prolific of fruits; the courses of the rivers, and the sea whose billows dash and break roaring against the crags! For the eye of the heavens blazes eternally with dazzling effulgence. Let us scatter and dissolve these dull mists that enfold us, and show ourselves to the earth in our immortal beauty.'"

The charm of this poetry lies in the truth as well as the beauty of its images; but the brief meteorological sketch which Aristophanes then gives, according to the theories of his epoch, is an example of the errors that must follow observation when not based, as it is to-day, upon knowledge of the physical laws the influence of which we are about to describe.

FORMATION OF THE CLOUDS AND MISTS.

The formation of mists and clouds is due to the presence of watery vapor in an atmosphere colder than the soil in which this vapor becomes visible, exactly like the steam that rises over boiling water.

The minute bodies of which the mist is composed are hollow globules, resembling soap-bubbles, or droplets of water, the diameter of which, measured through the microscope, is smaller in summer than in winter. This diameter increases also when rain is threatened.

Fogs being generally the result of the cooling of the atmosphere, and of the mingling of two currents of air of unequal temperature charged with moisture, they are seen forming, especially at morning and evening, and chiefly during the autumnal season, over rivers and lakes, the water of which is then much warmer than the atmosphere.

The formation of vapor is most abundant when the air is the dampest. Kaemtz, in his "Course of Meteorology," cites an observation made by the ancients in reference to the volcano of Stromboli: "When this volcano is covered with a cloud, the inhabitants of the Lipari Islands know that it will soon rain: but this does not happen, as they suppose, because the volcano is more active just before a shower; it is because the air, laden with watery vapor, cannot completely dissolve that which escapes from the crater."

Columns of mist ascend sometimes at certain points where the nature of the soil and vegetation give rise to a more active evaporation.

After heavy rains, and when the sun shines out again, these mists are seen appearing on the slopes of the mountains, where the ground is nearly always either arid or studded with woods, and following the undulations and accidents of the surface.

The same phenomenon occurs in Switzerland above lakes the temperature of which is more or less elevated, according to whether the streams that feed them do or do not issue from the region of eternal snow.

Mists form under circumstances also that are different only in appearance; for instance, when there is a thaw, and the air, laden with humidity, mingles with the colder air that is in contact with the ice that still covers the waters. The same cause produces the summer fogs seen along rivers, especially after heavy storms of rain.

INFLUENCE OF THE MARINE CURRENTS.

Marine currents of elevated temperature, such as the Gulf Stream, occasion frequent fogs on the colder coasts against which they beat. The dense fogs of Newfoundland and of the British Islands are ascribable to this influence, which has been noted in other regions—the Aleutian Isles, for instance, lying in the track of the great tepid current, analogous to the Gulf Stream, that crosses the North Pacific.

Lieutenant De Haven, of the United States Navy, during his expedition in search of Sir John Franklin, saw, at the northern extremity of Wellington Channel, a dense fog-bank motionless and suspended in the air—a water-sky, rising, to all appearance, above the Polar Sea, discovered in 1854 by Dr. Kane, the open waters of which are tempered by the submarine current found to exist in Davis's Strait.

EXTRAORDINARY MISTS.

Mists are sometimes of remarkable extent and duration. In 1821 and 1822 mists of this kind occurred in England and France, so dense that people could gaze upon the sun at noonday with the naked eye. In 1783 a similar fog covered nearly all Europe for the lapse of a month.

We read in a "Journal of the Reign of Henry III.," published in the French language:

"On Sunday, the 24th of January, 1588, there rose over the city of Paris and its environs so dense a fog, lasting from noon until the next day, as never was seen before within the memory of man. It was so black and thick that two persons walking together in the streets could not see each other, and were compelled to provide themselves with torches, in order to recognize one another, when it was not yet three o'clock. Very many wild geese, and other flying creatures of the air, were found where they had fallen bewildered in the courtyards of the houses, having dashed themselves against the buildings and the chimneys."

Captain Berg, a Russian officer, mentions a sort of mist that appears to rise from the sea in stormy weather, and is called *smoke*. We have repeatedly witnessed this phenomenon, which is ascribable partly to electricity. M. Peltier, the French savant, in one of his learned treatises, divides mists into two classes, viz., the electric and the non-electric. He explains the condition of the former by the combined influences of the earth and the higher regions of the atmosphere. Moreover, it has been ascertained that the electric fluid is constantly developed in the atmosphere surrounding cascades, where the water is incessantly reduced to fine spray, and this remarkable phenomenon might lead to a better determination of the influence, no longer to be denied, of atmospheric electricity on the formation of aqueous meteors.

Luminous mists are not uncommon. Mr. Wartmann, of Geneva, in a letter to M. Elie de Beaumont, given in the *Comptes Rendus* of the Academy of Sciences of Paris, for December 25, 1859, has described one of these strange meteors, which continued to appear for nine successive nights, viz., from the 18th to the 26th of November, 1859. The new moon, which was below the horizon, could not contribute to this phenomenon. The mist, which was very opaque, was still not moist enough to dampen the ground. It threw off light enough to enable one to distinguish the smaller articles in a room where the observer stood. A person who was proceeding on foot from Geneva to Annemasse, in Savoy, on the 22d of November, stated that he could see the road during the night as well as he could have done by the light of the moon.

Phosphorescent mists of the luminous order are usually dry mists, like those of 1783 and 1831, to which we shall refer again when we come to *igneous* meteors.

Certain mists that form over marshy plains have a peculiar odor, occasioned probably by the miasma which they contain and bear along with them.

In regions where it seldom rains, as for instance

at Lima and around it, the mists caused by local circumstances last sometimes for a part of the year, serving to moisten the soil and maintain the freshness of the vegetation.

Mists are often seen forming over hollows where the water is nearly always colder than the air, and determines the collection of vapor above it. Humboldt states that in the South Sea Islands the shape of these mists frequently reproduces that of the hollows exactly.

APPEARANCE AND MOTION OF THE CLOUDS.

The appearance and movements of the clouds, the formation of which is due to the same causes that produce the mists, are to be numbered among the chief indications that announce to us the changes brought about in the aërial ocean by the variations of electric tension, temperature, and humidity.

Mountain-summits are often enveloped in clouds produced by the damp air, and by the watery vapor that condenses by degrees as it rises toward those colder regions. These clouds are very frequently observed to disperse, as they get farther away from the mountain-tops and encounter air-currents of a more elevated temperature.

" Often," says Kaemtz, " dark clouds pass rapidly over the Hospice of Saint Gothard and precipitate themselves in heavy masses into the Val Tremola. One would think, to look at them, that all Lombardy was about to be buried under a dense fog; but, at the outlet of the Val Tremola, it is already dispersed by the warm currents of air ascending."

During very violent winds, clouds are seen, in consequence of like circumstances, clinging to the peaks of mountain-ridges, and apparently motionless, while around those peaks the intervals remain perfectly clear.

The appearance of remarkable clouds suspended on the summits of lofty mountains sometimes announces tempests, always preceded by atmospheric variations, which practice in observing natural signs teaches us to recognize. Thus, the people of the Cape of Good Hope prognosticate tempests from the southwest (so formidable in their latitudes) whenever they see a compact, lead-colored cloud gathering around the summits of their highlands, and particularly on Table Mountain.

ICE-CLOUDS.

The mists that form on the surface of the ground, either in the depths of valleys or on the heights, become clouds whenever, carried upward by ascending currents, they remain suspended in the atmosphere above us. Clouds are also formed directly in the air by the meeting of two winds laden with moisture and of unequal temperature, or by the condensation of copious vapors which rise toward the colder regions of the atmosphere.

Sometimes there are several beds of cloud resting one above the other, and, generally, the whiter they look, the higher they are.

The temperature of the regions that the clouds ascend to is often several degrees below zero, and, as may readily be understood, they are then composed of icy particles, like the fine needles of the mists that ascend in fleecy masses during severe cold weather, and are often seen glistening in the sunlight.

In reference to this subject we shall cite an important observation that concerns meteorology in the highest degree. It was enunciated in a remarkable lecture on "the influence exerted upon vegetation by the atmosphere."

The lecture in question was delivered by one of the most learned and courageous scientific experimentalists of France, Professor J. A. Barral, before the Chemical Society of Paris.

"On July 25, 1850, my friend M. Bixio and

I were fortunate enough to ascend in a balloon beyond the stratum attained by Gay-Lussac in 1804, and some surprise was manifested that we, in the midst of a violently-agitated atmosphere, and in the bosom of a vast ice-cloud, should have found 39°.7 (by the aid of numerous and delicate instruments graduated by M. Regnault), or, in other words, the temperature at which mercury solidifies, in the same region where Gay-Lussac had noted only 9°.5, when the air was calm and the sky clear. This surprise had no other basis than a defective interpretation of the facts already established. At the present day we have to admit that, even in the very highest regions of the atmosphere that men have reached, there are considerable variations in the temperature of the air as well as upon the surface of the earth. A circumstance no less remarkable is, that, in midsummer, clouds of more than four thousand yards in thickness, composed of numberless little needles of ice, may be seen gliding above our heads at a velocity of at least thirty miles an hour. In those regions where eternal silence reigns, and where all life has ceased, are condensed, along with the last watery molecules that have mounted from the bosom of the earth and the clouds, those innumerable exhalations which we are wont to term the impurities of the atmosphere. The matter contained in them descends again with the rain, the hail, and the snow, to the surface of our planet, where it is disseminated, and conveys to the barrenest rock the elements necessary to support vegetation, which may thus develop and distribute themselves in nearly every latitude, whatever may be the character of the soil that receives the fertilizing shower. The lower aërial strata that touch the surface of the solid crust of our globe, and the doubly extensive surface of its seas and oceans, after having become laden with various materials, dilate by the effect of heat, and then ascend until they meet the chill that condenses them in the higher regions, and causes them to fall again to the surface. Thus a continual rising and falling motion is produced in that atmospheric belt, between four and five miles in thickness, which we have been able to sound. The rain and the snow are formed, and, borne far away from the spot which saw the birth of the embryo cloud, they go forth to fertilize distant plains by besprinkling them with water that is saturated with a new air."

In England the latest winter ascensions of a learned aëronaut, Mr. Glaisher, enabled him to detect, at an elevation where the temperature was very low during the summer ascensions, a current of warm air, seven hundred yards in thickness, charged with vapor. The latter soon afterward descended upon the city of London and enveloped it in a dense fog.

These interesting observations go to prove that the loftier regions of the atmosphere are traversed, like the depths of the ocean, by great currents of unequal temperature, which, no doubt, contribute to the maintenance of a general system of aërial circulation, and which, sometimes descending to the surface of the earth, there produce those great changes of temperature that meteorological observation will one day, perhaps, enable us to foresee with sufficient accuracy.

THE FORMS OF THE CLOUDS.

The causes which determine the forms, the color, and the elevation of the clouds, are not yet known. The double action of the currents of warm air which ascend from the earth in the daytime and the horizontal currents, suffices to explain the suspension in the atmosphere of the visible vapors, heavier as the latter are than the medium in which they float. According to Presnel, the solar heat absorbed by the clouds makes a sort of balloon of them, which rises the higher according to the greater elevation of the temperature. It is owing to these influences that clouds are generally higher at noon than toward evening.

M. Jamin, in his course of lectures at the Sorbonne, has demonstrated that the aqueous particles whose aggregation makes a cloud, are in the condition of full droplets, and that, when the radius of these droplets is sufficiently small, but little effort is required to sustain them at certain heights. This effort is always supplied by the continual displacements going on in the atmosphere.

Dr. Howard, a learned English writer on physical and meteorological science, was the first who distinguished in the clouds the four leading forms of *Cirrus*, *Stratus*, *Nimbus*, and *Cumulus*. He classifies them in his " Essay on the Modifications of Clouds, and on the Principles of their Production, Suspension, and Destruction," published at London in 1802.

The *cirrus* consists of thin, transparent clouds, which look like delicate plumes, and are always seen at a great height. They are sometimes observed in parallel bands, or in filaments, stretching north and south, appearing to diverge from one point on the horizon and to converge toward another diametrically opposite. "Many meteorologists," says M. Charles Martins, "for instance,

FORMS OF THE CLOUDS—THE CIRRUS, OR CAT-TAILS.

Howard, Forster, Peltier, and others, think that the cirri serve as conductors between two distant

STRATUS.

centres of electricity of different poles, in which the fluid is seeking an equilibrium, and that the flexibility of the clouds at length gives them the rectilinear form required by the necessity for the shortest possible transit from one focus to the other. The whiteness of the cirri arises from the icy particles and snow-flakes of which they are composed. Their peculiar appearance has earned for them the various titles of "*cat-tails*,"

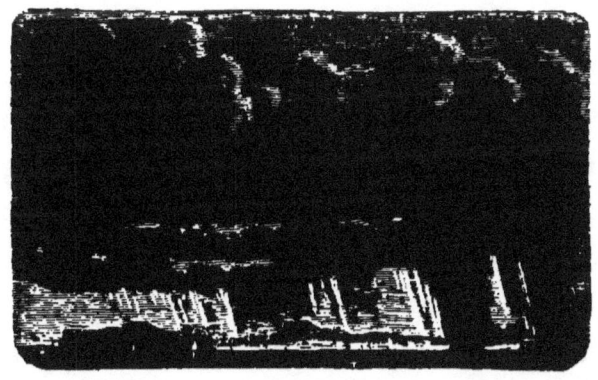

NIMBUS.

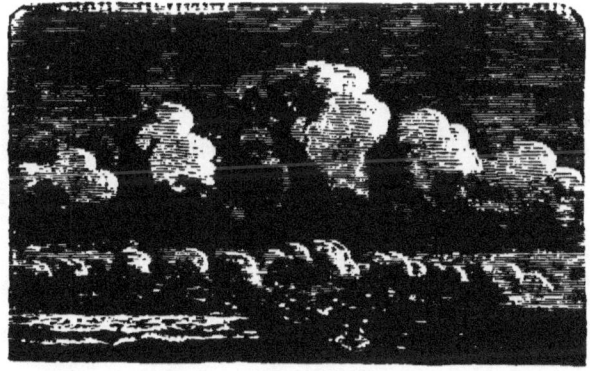

CUMULUS.

"*horse-tails,*" "*mackerel-sky,*" etc. They nearly always portend a change of weather.

The *stratus* is the long horizontal belt of smoke-colored clouds that often extends across the horizon at sunset, and that may be seen forming, on fine summer evenings, above expanses of water and damp meadows. These cloudy bands may be thick and extensive enough to cover the sky, but they never yield rain.

The *nimbus* is a mass of dense, black clouds, with jagged borders, which announce rain or storm. Hence a cloud of any kind resolving itself into rain always takes the form of the nimbus.

The *cumulus* consists of what we may term "the fine-weather clouds." Their whiteness, which contrasts with the blue of the sky; their rounded, half-spherical forms; their well-defined outlines, make it easy to distinguish them. Piled up on the horizon, they frequently assume the shape of lofty snow-clad mountains, and when they are seen to darken at the same time that the lower bed of the cloud spreads out into a *stratus*, rain may be expected.

The great poet Goethe, who was also a distinguished naturalist, has left us some remarkable points relating to meteorology. We will quote a passage from one of his learned essays on the subject, as epitomized by the French *savant* Martins, who has edited the great German's scientific lucubrations on natural history:

"When Goethe was made acquainted with Howard's theory, he hastened to verify its principles, and to that end undertook a series of experiments and observations. These observations were chiefly made during the course of a journey in Bohemia, between the 23d of April, 1820, and the 28th of May in the same year. They were accompanied by considerations of a general character, to which we would, for a moment, call attention.

" Goethe, in common with many other meteorologists, distinguishes three regions in the atmosphere: the most elevated is characterized by its dryness; it therefore tends to absorb the moisture of the lower strata; and in this region the sky is clear, or covered with a few clouds disposed in the cirrus form. Goethe did not remark that, in the icy heights of the atmosphere, the vapors become converted into snow, and that the cirrus is made up of masses of snow-flakes. In the intermediate regions we find the cumulus, whose strange and ever-varying forms have become the object of many superstitious notions among the dwellers in mountainous districts. Below the cirrus and the cumulus extends the stratus, which occupies the lowest part of the upper atmosphere.

"The higher and the lower regions are in a state of perpetual conflict. Sometimes the upper regions prevail, and the cumuli, being rent asunder, rise and are scattered abroad in the form of fleecy particles. Sometimes, on the other hand, the lower region is the more powerful; then, the *cumulus* is lengthened out to a *stratus*, and the heaped-up mass of clouds becomes a *nimbus* big with rain. The formation of clouds may take an opposite course: dense fogs ascend from the earth in the shape of elongated *strata*, and group themselves into thick cumuli, or separate and form the cirrus. Goethe holds persistently to this conflict between the higher and lower regions of the atmosphere, and claims to have noticed that the east and north winds coöperate with the action of the upper regions, and those of the west and south with the action of the lower layers."

DISTRIBUTION OF THE CLOUDS.—THE CLOUD-RING.

The distribution of the clouds in different parts of the globe has been too imperfectly observed to enable us to deduce any general laws therefrom. Moreover, this distribution is evidently in direct relation to the quantity of rain that falls in each region, and we shall presently sum up the data thus far obtained in reference to that branch of meteorology which relates directly to cultivation and to the fertility of the soil.

This fertility is not due merely to the beneficent action of the rain that waters our fields, nor to the snow that protects them in winter. The clouds, in spreading their mantle over the earth, keep in its heat or prevent excessive drought, and, as Maury has well said, in his "Physical Geography and Meteorology of the Sea, " "when their task is accomplished at one point, the winds bear them away, to perform the same regulating function elsewhere."

In the zone of the equatorial calms one can best appreciate this influence of the clouds upon climate and vegetation. While in the region of the trade-winds, both north and south of the equator, the sky is usually clear or dotted with light clouds; we, on the contrary, when approaching the zone of calms, see the sky become obscured and covered with dense vapors, arising from the masses of air saturated with moisture which the trade-winds continually sweep into that zone. The dais or disk of clouds thus formed extends around the globe like a ring, or belt, which is carried from the north to the south, or from the south to the north, within certain limits, according to the season, alternately protecting the different parallels that it covers from the blaze of the sun, and bringing them rain at given periods.

INFLUENCE OF MOUNTAINS.—THE SPECTRE OF THE BROCKEN.

We have already referred to the influence exerted by mountains on the condensation of vapors. M. de Gasparin, in his "Rural Meteorology," cites quite a remarkable observation in connection with this subject. "It is known," says he," that the narrow passage leading into the harbor of Plymouth is bounded on the east and west by two promontories covered with woods. J. Harvey has noticed that a dense and quite compact cloud, coming from the west, disappeared in passing over the strait and formed again upon reaching the opposite point of land."

The abundance of clouds in mountainous countries, their capricious forms, and frequently strange distortions, have furnished geniuses and poets with beautiful similes. Popular traditions show us that these natural phenomena have long been the source of superstitions that have not yet entirely died out. Thus, in certain parts of the

1

THE SPECTRE OF THE BROCKEN.

Vosges Mountains, the long, black trains of clouds that unroll and wind fiercely down through the deep gorges, at the approach of storms, still inspire terror, as a token of the presence of evil spirits sweeping by with the tempest.

A wonderful phenomenon, the Spectre of the Brocken, was long explained by a superstitious peasantry as the work of direct supernatural intervention. One of the best descriptions of this phenomenon was given by Mr. Hane, who witnessed it on May 25, 1797: "After having scaled the summit of the mountain more than thirty times, in vain, at last he had the good fortune to see the object of his curiosity. The sun rose at about four o'clock in the morning, and the weather was fine. The wind was driving before it toward the west masses of transparent vapor, which had not yet had time to condense into clouds. About a quarter-past four, the traveller saw, in the direction of Achtermannshohe, a human figure of enormous dimensions. A gust of wind having nearly blown away Mr. Hane's hat, he quickly put up his hand to retain it, and the strange figure made the same gesture. Mr. Hane then immediately made another motion, stooping downward, and this act was likewise reproduced by the spectre. Another person joined Mr. Hane, at this moment, and the two gentlemen, placing themself together on the very spot from which the apparition had been noticed, looked toward Achtermannshohe, but saw nothing. However, a little while afterward, two colossal figures appeared in the same direction imitating the motions and gestures of the two observers, and then disappeared. They showed themselves again, a little later, accompanied by a third figure. Sometimes these shapes were feeble and indistinct; at others they were very intensely marked and their outlines sharply defined. The reader will have guessed that the phenomenon was produced by the shadow of the spectators projected on a cloud. The third figure was undoubtedly due to a third person half hidden behind some broken mass of rock."

During his journey with La Condamine among the Cordilleras, Bouguer, a member of the French Academy of Sciences, sent out with the former to South America to measure a degree of the earth's surface, witnessed a phenomenon, similar to the one just described, from the summit of Pambamarca:

" What astonished us," says he, " was that the head of the shadow was adorned with a halo formed of three or four small concentric crowns of very vivid color, each one with the same variety as the first rainbow, the red on the outside. This made a sort of apotheosis for each spectator, and I must not forget to add that each of them tranquilly enjoyed the pleasure of seeing himself decorated with all these crowns, without even catching a glimpse of those of his neighbors."

Kaemtz has verified the same thing on the Alps. So soon as the shadow was projected on a cloud, the head was seen surrounded by a luminous halo. Scoresby in the polar regions, Ramond in the Pyrenees, and De Saussure, have all seen and described this curious phenomenon, which is known under the name of *Anthelia*.

Sometimes it is observed under more ordinary circumstances, at the rising and the setting of the sun, when fogs are resting on the ground. Frequently the aërial figure, the head of which is almost always surrounded with luminous rays, is no larger than life. It may be readily conceived that such apparitions gave rise to the quaint legends heard in different countries, particularly in mountainous regions where the lofty summits, crowned with clouds of varying outline and ever-changing colors, have played so grand a part in the composition of religious fables.

When the sun is just at the horizon, one may,

if standing close to a railway, see the shadows of the telegraph-posts appear on the long pennant of white steam that rises from the locomotive, and floats over the train. Aëronauts often see the magnified image of their balloon upon the clouds, in the elevated regions through which they pass. The phenomenon is in every case of the same general nature as the famous Spectre of the Brocken.

THE SHADOW OF MONT BLANC.

When the spectator happens to be standing on the summit of a very high mountain, the shadow projected by the setting sun is directed upward to the sky, and sometimes produces a magnificent phenomenon, which was observed by Messrs. Bravais and Martins in one of their scientific excursions to Mont Blanc. M. Bravais has given the following description of it:

"As the sun was approaching the moment of his setting, we looked in the direction opposite to the luminary, and beheld, not without some surprise, the shadow of Mont Blanc defined upon the snow-clad mountains in the eastern part of the panorama before us. It gradually rose in the atmosphere until it attained the height of an entire degree, remaining all the while distinctly visible.

"The air above the apex of the shadow was

tinged with that purply rose-color, which one sees, in fine sunsets, suffusing the loftiest peaks. The edge of this color presented a zone of deeper intensity, and that continuous bordering enhanced the splendor of the phenomenon.

"Let any one imagine the mountains in the great valley of Aosta projecting their shadows at one and the same moment upon the atmosphere, the lower part dark with a slight greenish tinge, and, above each of these shadows, a breadth of purply rose-color, with a belt of deep rosy-red separating it from them; let him add to that the sharp uprightness of the cones and peaks in the shadow, especially of their uppermost ridges, and, finally, the effects of perspective, making all these lines converge one upon the other toward the very summit of the shadow of Mont Blanc, that is to say, toward that point in the sky where the shadows of our bodies should be. Even then he will have but an incomplete idea of the richness of the meteorological phenomenon that developed itself before us for some moments. It seemed as though an invisible being were in a throne girt round with fire, and that, on their knees, angels with glittering wings were worshipping him, all bending their forms toward him. At the sight of a spectacle so magnificent our arms and those of our guides dropped motionless, and cries of enthusiasm escaped our lips. I have seen the superb aurora borealis of the north, with its crowns in the zenith, and its variegated wavering colonnades of pillars, far surpassing the finest devices of our pyrotechnists, but the spectacle presented by the shadow of Mont Blanc, in my opinion, went beyond them all."

CHAPTER III.

RAIN, SNOW, AND HAIL.

Dew.—White Frost.—The Distribution of Rain on the Surface of the Globe.—The Great Rains of India.—Regions without Rain.—Influence of Forests.—The Softening of Climates—Forms of the Snow.—Flowers under the Snow.—Glaciers and Rivers.—Hail.

DEW AND WHITE FROST.

Dew—the bright deposit of limpid little drops which glisten in the morning light on the foliage, like pearls and diamonds—is caused by the condensation of atmospheric vapor on substances sufficiently cooled during the night by radiation, or the loss of heat through the air. Doctor Wells, an English physician, was the first to give this explanation, after a great number of experiments.

A lock of very dry wool weighing 10 grains, placed upon a plank sustained by four uprights, increased its weight only two grains by moisture, while a similar lock placed above it gained 14 grains, and another, laid on the grass, increased

16 grains. Thermometers substituted for these locks of wool exhibited the lowest range where the dew fell the most copiously. On the other hand, substances that do not so readily part with their caloric, such as the metals, remained dry, while others of greater radiating power lying close beside them were covered with dew. A clear sky was found to be favorable to the cooling process, and consequently to the deposit of dew; and the passing of a cloud, which gives heat for heat, was sufficient to arrest the phenomenon. Moreover, it was observed that less dew formed in the depth of valleys than on the tops of hills, from which a greater extent of clear sky could be perceived.

When the nocturnal radiation causes the temperature of a body to descend below zero, the watery vapor condenses into ice, and *white frost* is deposited instead of dew. A custom prevalent in India may serve to give an idea of the power of this cooling process. Ice is habitually procured there by exposing shallow pails, filled with water, and isolated from the terrestrial heat by layers of loose straw laid beneath them, in some open place, during very clear nights. Under these conditions the temperature of water has been known to fall 17 degrees.

In order to protect plants from the disastrous

effects of these frosts, it suffices to arrange a horizontal screen about two yards above the ground, to prevent radiation. In the open field, during the clear nights of the end of April and the beginning of May, the cold often destroys the buds of plants. This occurs when the moon shines in an unclouded sky, but, should the latter be obscured, no such bad effects are observed.

The *russet or "red moon"* is thus explained: The luminary of night is often most wrongfully blamed by country-people, since it is really the serenity of the sky which is the cause of the hurtful chill, and the consequent loss of crops.

THE DISTRIBUTION OF RAIN ON THE GLOBE'S SURFACE.

The refreshing stimulus extended to plants by fogs and dew is but temporary. A humidity much more abundant is required by them. Although there are very heavy dews in Egypt, the vegetation of that country would soon disappear were it not that the inundations of the Nile make up for the extreme rarity of rain. In years when the overflow is but limited, those districts which it does not touch remain sterile. Farmers everywhere, whether fearing an excess of moisture or of drought, attach great importance to the rain, its quantity and its distribution throughout the seasons of the year.

Rain falls sometimes when no cloud is visible, and the sky is perfectly clear. Various observations of this nature are cited by Humboldt and Arago. "The night was fine," says a *savant* of Geneva, "and the stars were shining with their ordinary brightness, when a rain composed of large, tepid drops fell over the city for six minutes." The same phenomenon is reported by an eye-witness to have taken place at Constantine at noon, and with the sky magnificently blue and clear.

But usually it is after having passed through the cloudy form that the moisture of the atmosphere precipitates itself, and the indications contained in the preceding chapter give the first elements of the geographical distribution of rain.

To commence with, we have the equatorial zone, enveloped in its girdle of clouds, formed not only by the vapors arising from the warm waters of the ocean carried up by powerful ascending currents, but also by those that the trade-winds sweep thither from north and south. This is a region where rain falls every day and in great abundance, the mixture of the masses of saturated air with the cold atmospheric layers taking place continually under a very hot sun. Mention has been made of calms sufficiently prolonged and accompanied by rains heavy enough to make the water fresh on the surface of the sea. The mariner is shy of these latitudes, where the tepid and heavy atmosphere causes an irresistible languor and develops dangerous diseases. Storms are so frequent there that it is rarely one does not hear the thunder rumbling above the dense clouds with an echo like the fiercest electric explosions among mountains. The familiar expression *blacking-pot*, so often on the lips of sailors, very appropriately conveys the effect of the sombre belt thus described after the unvarying blue of the trade-wind skies.

All the vapor disengaged in this immense equatorial boiler does not fall in rain at the same place. Atmospheric currents higher up than the trade-winds carry it toward the two poles. They come in contact with the surface of the earth in a region the limits of which vary with the annual advance of the sun, like those of the equatorial belt of clouds, and which, as a general thing, is fixed in the tropics. Places situated in this region have periodical rainy seasons called *winterings*.

In our temperate latitudes, the commingling

of layers which produces the rain ceases to be the result of ascending currents meeting with the upper cold air. It is produced by horizontal currents, the direction of which is generally opposite to each other. This rain falls at all periods of the year.

At the 60th degree of latitude we reach the circumpolar zone, where no rain falls in winter, owing to the extreme rarefaction of the limpid atmosphere, which extends over the immense expanse of snow, and no fogs are seen to form, excepting in those regions where the water is open.

If we compare the system of the circulation of the waters upon the surface of the globe to an alembic with the fire at the equator, we shall see that the regions outside of the tropics perform the part of condensers. Lieutenant Maury has very strikingly illustrated the functions of this admirable apparatus. "The average amount of rain that falls annually upon the surface of our globe," he says, "has been estimated at 1.5 yards in depth; Thus, then, to raise enough of water from the ocean, every year, in the form of vapor, to cover the earth with a spherical coating 1.5 yards deep; to carry that watery vapor from one zone to another, and then to precipitate it in different forms at certain determinate points at chosen epochs, and in appropriate quantities, such are the functions of the great atmospheric machine. The water vaporized in this manner being taken principally from the torrid zone, the atmosphere in that zone alone must absorb a liquid mass of nearly 5 yards in thickness, and 3,000 marine miles in breadth, upon a development of 24,000 miles; raise it as high as the clouds, and then let it fall again upon the earth. This it must, moreover, do every year! What a wondrous and powerful mechanism, then, is this atmosphere of ours, and how harmoniously its different elements must be combined in order that this work, which overwhelms the imagination, may be carried on without the slightest disarrangement ever manifesting itself in a totality of functions as complex as they are varied!"

THE GREAT RAINS OF INDIA.

The regions where the monsoons prevail have an exceptional pluvial arrangement. In the month of April, the season of the northeast trade-winds closes in India. The vast deserts of Central Asia, heated by the sun, give a sort of breathing aspiration that produces the southwest monsoons. Laden with the vapors of the ocean and of the Arabian Gulf, these winds strike the Ghaut range of mountains at right angles, and there deposit an extraordinary quantity of rain, which Johnson tells us has been known to attain the enormous measurement of $14\frac{1}{2}$ inches in a single day. They then diverge toward the Himalayas, where the temperature is lower than on the summits of the Ghauts. There they abandon in the form of snow and rain nearly all the moisture with which they were charged, and thus it happens that, when they reach the arid wastes beyond those mountains, they rarely have enough vapor left to form clouds. It is at Cherrapondschi, among the Himalayas, that the maximum of rain-fall, viz., 17 yards per annum, has been found for the entire globe.

Owing to these rains, vegetation attains a prodigious development in India; but they are accompanied by all sorts of pests, as Mr. D. Warren graphically describes them in his work on British India.

"A suffocating calm," he says, "which prevails particularly about the end of the great heats, precedes the setting in of the southern monsoon. With the end of May come on the first storms, which are brief, but of extreme violence. Thunder is heard in the distance at intervals; the sun sets in a bed of clouds, and every evening the lightnings illuminate all points of the horizon.

THE GREAT RAINS OF INDIA. 69

The rain falls, for half an hour, in torrents; after a few days it lasts longer, and toward the middle of June it rules the entire day, for, when it is not actually raining, the sky is at least covered with a dense and threatening curtain of clouds. It rains sometimes, particularly in July, for thirty or forty hours consecutively, and then not in fine lines, broken and almost imperceptible, as in our climates, but in straight, parallel streaks, and frequently like a sheet of water coming down all at once with the fury and impetuosity of a cascade.

"The miserable clay-huts of the natives become thoroughly soaked under this continual avalanche; their roofs fall in and bury them, or, at all events, escaping that easier fate, they find themselves exposed to all the rigors of the open air, and perish in great numbers. This is the period of widespread distress, which does not spare even the nabob and the conqueror; and the very reptiles, those of the most hateful species, like the rest, inundated in their holes, dart to the surface of the soil and seek an asylum among the dwellings of men. Numerous varieties of snakes, centipedes, and scorpions, climb your stairs, invade your houses, and glide into every room. It is impossible to take a step in one's bedchamber at night without a light, unless one is prepared to run the risk of a sting that may prove fatal. The utmost distrust must be felt of every thing that one touches; a cruel bite may kill you from the inside of a boot or a sleeve. For some time you lead a life of continual alarm and disgusting contacts; but these annoyances are not of long duration. The monsoon begins to decline in the month of August, and dies away in the first days of September. The five months that follow, until the beginning of February, are delicious, and make one forget those that went before; there is rapture in the mere fact of existence, the air is so fresh and the face of Nature so lovely."

REGIONS WITHOUT RAIN.

There are parts of the globe's surface where rain is almost unknown. Such are the coasts of Peru, and it is easy to discover the reason. They lie within the sweep of the southeast trade-winds. The latter traverse the Atlantic and there become laden with vapors, which they then deposit on their trip across the American Continent, where the rain feeds the sources of the Rio de la Plata and the southern affluents of the Amazon. Then, they pass on to the snowy peaks of the Cordilleras, where the low temperature completely divests them of the moisture they may still have retained. We need not be surprised, then, that they are dry and cold when they sweep down the western slope of the Andes, and remain so until they meet the waters of the Pacific Ocean.

A large part of Australia also is in the track of the southeast trade-winds, and should have large rivers, like that intertropical portion of South America just mentioned; but the contrary is the case. Maury explains this difference by the relations that exist between the direction of the winds and that of the coasts. "In Australia," he says, "the eastern coast runs in the direction of the trade-winds, while in South America it is perpendicular to that line. Consequently, in Australia, these winds only fringe the coast, so to speak, with their vapors, and dispense their rains over these parched lands so sparingly, that the trees, in order to retain the small amount of moisture allotted to them, are obliged to arrange their leaves in the same line as the rays of the sun, since, if they were in the natural position, they would be too quickly dried up. On the contrary, in South America, where the winds blow in a direction perpendicular to the shore, and cause the humidity with which they are charged to penetrate to the heart of the country, one sees the leaves striving, as it were, to reach the sun's rays and present themselves to them in their fullest development."

The Desert of Sahara, situated in the domain of the trade-winds that cross the land only, is denied rain entirely, and shows us what our globe would be without the magnificent reservoir of the ocean. From the immense sandy plains of Africa there rises only a column of burning air, while not even a drop of dew falls to moisten the parched surface and there develop vegetation.

THE INFLUENCE OF FORESTS.

The influence of forests, in reference to rain, has been established by numerous observations. Columbus mentions it in his "Journal of the Voyage to America," where he attributes to the density and extent of the forests that covered the mountain-sides the abundance of rain to which he was so long exposed while coasting along the shores of Jamaica. He remarks that "formerly rain was no less abundant at Madeira and on the Canaries and Azores, but since the trees that gave shade have been cut down, it has become much less frequent in those countries."

Humboldt demonstrates that there exists a

frigorific radiation above wooded regions, that must condense the vapors. The summits of mountains covered with forests become enveloped with mists oftener than those of mountains that are bare, and springs of water are more frequently found among them. Numerous plantations of trees in Egypt have caused the rains that had totally ceased to reappear—a fact that deserves especial mention. In some parts of the Antilles the clearing of portions of the soil has diminished the quantity of rain, and the watercourses have lost their abundance.

At Porto Rico a different plan has been pursued. A decree of the King of Spain prescribed that, every time a tree should be cut down, three should be planted for it, and the country has consequently retained its high fertility. The beauty of the soil and the abundance of water have left the land more productive than on the adjacent islands.

We extract from the scientific work of M. Boussingault a passage confirming the existence of similar relations between the clearing away of the woods and the quantity of water: "In the valley of Cauca," he says, "it is well known that such and such a district, whose soil and medium temperature are favorable to the cultivation of the cacao-tree, still gives no good result if the latter be placed too near to the forest. But, when these forest-lands are cleared, and transformed to fields of yucca, sugar-cane, and maize, the cacao-tree flourishes remarkably. The following fact was obtained from Don Sebastian Marisansena, a resident of Cartago. Having procured the title of *capitan poblador* to found a village at La Balsá, at the foot of the Quindin range, he began by putting in a plantation of cocoa-trees. During the first ten years the crops amounted to little or nothing, because the rains were too frequent. The *hacienda*, or farm, began to be productive only when the inhabitants of La Balsá were numerous enough to make the clearings extensive. Then at length the sun could ripen the cacao. In 1816, political events led to a large emigration of the people, only the negroes remaining on the farm. Six years later, the surrounding fields were again transformed to forests; the crops diminished more and more, and in 1827, when I passed through La Balsá, they had not gathered any cacao for three years."

AMELIORATION OF CLIMATE.

The clouds when they dissolve in rain restore to the atmosphere all the heat that was taken up in forming them. Every one may have observed the increased mildness of the atmosphere after a shower of some duration. This circumstance powerfully affects the climates of the higher latitudes, especially in the southern hemisphere, where the counter trade-winds of the northwest condense their abundant vapors. It has been observed that, relatively to their position, the southern Shetlands have no very cold winters; a fact undoubtedly due to the great quantity of heat disengaged during the rains.

The quantity of rain that falls on the western slope of the Patagonian Andes (and, according to Admiral Fitzroy, it amounts to more than four yards in forty days) imparts a remarkable degree of heat to the winds that descend upon the other slope. It is to them, as well as to a feeble oceanic current, that the extraordinary climate of the Falkland Islands is to be attributed. These islands are in a latitude corresponding to the rude regions of Labrador, and yet cattle pass the winter there in the midst of fine pasture.

In North America, at the base and on the slopes of the Rocky Mountains, where the Missouri takes its rise, there is a phenomenon observable that must be ascribed to the heat disengaged by the great condensation that takes place when the western winds of the Pacific strike the summits of the chain. In winter, navigation is open on the upper part of the river, while lower down it is entirely closed by the ice. At a very considerable elevation, a spring temperature is enjoyed, and the country is covered with rich verdure, at the very moment when the severest cold prevails in the distant plains below.

FORMS OF THE SNOW.

When a current of very cold air penetrates to a warm apartment suddenly, it may produce snow, if the room be full of watery vapor. The story is told that, upon one occasion in St. Petersburg, a pane of glass was accidentally broken in the window of a saloon where a large party was assembled, and a gust of wind bursting in through the orifice, congealed the vapors of the room and scattered them over the astonished guests in the shape of snow-flakes. Similar effects have been noticed in Siberia and Nova Zembla.

Whenever the temperature of the clouds falls below zero, their drops congeal and form snow, which then falls through the air in flakes until it strikes the ground. These flakes, when caught upon a black surface and examined through the microscope, exhibit a remarkable regularity of form that long since attracted the attention of observers. Kepler speaks of their structure with lively admiration, and, since his day, these graceful crystallizations have been described with care.

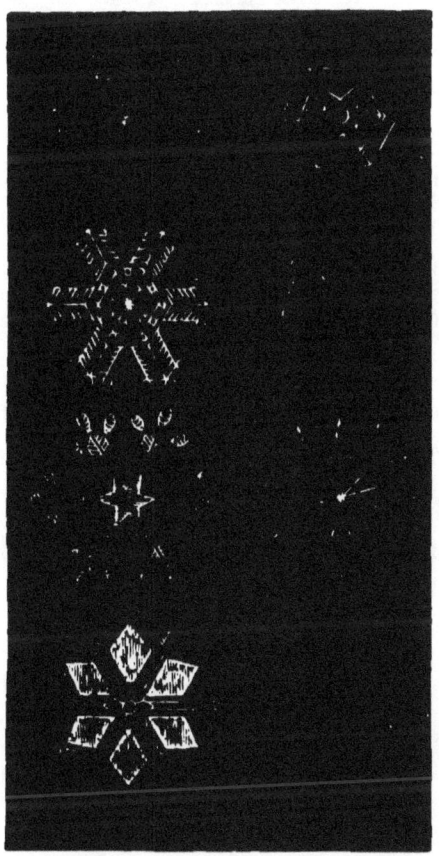

FORMS OF SNOW-CRYSTALS.

Yet, notwithstanding their great variety, they depend upon extremely simple laws. "These snow crystals," says Tyndall, "being formed in a calm atmosphere, are constructed on the same model: their molecules group together to form hexagonal stars. From a central nucleus project six needles that, together, form an angle of 60 degrees. From these central needles there shoot out other smaller ones to the right and the left, in their turn describing with infallible fidelity their angle of 60 degrees. These six-leaved flowers assume the most varied and wondrous forms. They are patterned in the finest gauzy films, and all around their angles are sometimes seen rosettes of still more microscopic dimensions. Beauty superadds itself to beauty, as though, when once at work, Nature took pleasure in showing, even in the narrowest sphere, the omnipotence of her resources." The temperature, the humidity, the degree of motion in the air, modify these crystallized figures. Flakes that fall at the same time generally have the same shape; but, when there is an interval between the falls, a new variety is found each time.

FLOWERS UNDER THE SNOW.

In years when the snow has remained long upon the ground, the watercourses are more abundant, and the harvests more certain. Winters at the North without snow are calamities equalled only by springs at the South without rain. Snow acts as a covering, or screen, which, in sheltering the soil, prevents it from being thoroughly congealed, by the radiation of all its caloric into space, in clear, cold nights; and then, when the thaw comes, it fully saturates the ground.

Between the eternal snows that cover the tops of the Pyrenees and the Alps, and the slopes at their foot, where the vine flourishes, there is a region in which the snow melts at different seasons, according to its elevation; but, in all places, even at great heights, where it remains for six or eight months, when it does disappear it leaves the soil covered with rich herbage that vegetated under its shelter, and that offers an abundant pasture to the flocks and herds. The green sward thus strengthened is immediately enamelled with a multitude of lovely flowers that had budded beneath the snow. The attempt had often been made, but in vain, to acclimate these Alpine plants in our gardens, when a florist conceived the idea, which seemed odd enough at first, to place them, during the winter, between the orange and pomegranate trees in his hot-house. The hardy plants brought from a rude region, where the climate is similar to that of Siberia, and where the mercury sinks to 30° below zero, were perfectly preserved by the process. This was because they found in the hot-house the conditions provided for them by the thick covering of snow that shielded them in their natural haunts. By its diminutive conducting power, the covering in question shelters them from cold, and, above all, from those abrupt changes of temperature that are so injurious to frail organizations. By analogy we may infer how grain is protected by the snow in the furrows of our fields.

GLACIERS AND RIVERS.

An admirable arrangement in the glaciers of the Alps has been made apparent by a series of observations, carefully pursued for several years consecutively, in regard to the mean depth of water in the rivers flowing from them, in each month of the year. "Since much less rain falls in summer than in other seasons," says Jean Reynaud, "and since it evaporates again almost immediately, all the small streams diminish in volume, and some are even dried up altogether; thus, at last, the main watercourses do not receive from their tributaries sufficient aliment to sustain them. But Nature has arranged a peculiar class of tributaries for rivers important enough to require such special provision, and these yield them all the more in proportion as their ordinary resources diminish, and *vice versa*. These are the streamlets that flow from the glaciers; and the immensity of the process required to supply them will be comprehended at once, when we reflect that they must necessarily be raised from the mountains above the clouds, in order to take their rise where they do. None but regions lifted up to those prodigious elevations would be in a position to accumulate such a quantity of snow and ice, and to retain enough of it during the summer, allowing it to melt, little by little. Thus, the hotter the summer and the more extreme the drought in the watercourses of the plains, only the more rapidly and copiously will the deposits of ice heaped up at the fountain-head be made to melt. Consequently the mountain-brooks will be the fullest at the very moment when the others will be most completely exhausted. On the other hand, in spring and autumn, when the abundance of rain causes the streamlets of the valley and the plain to swell in every direction, and tends to raise the rivers above their regular beds, the glaciers, receiving less heat, feed the rills that flow from them less lavishly, and an actual dryness results, so far as they are concerned, which counterbalances the humidity of the regions lower down. The general result is, that the rivers which are subject solely to the influence of the glaciers are full in summer and shallow in winter; while those which are cut off from all connection with the reservoirs of the high regions, and are dependent upon the rains alone, have the most water during the cold season and the least in the hot months. Finally, those that have the aid of both the glaciers and the rain, at different times, along with ordinary tributaries and such as flow from the high mountains, have, other things being equal, a more even and steady supply of water than the rest."

HAIL.

Hail is a shower of globules of ice, the size of which usually varies from that of a pea to that of a hickory-nut, but sometimes attains the dimensions of an egg, and even of an ordinary apple. It has been remarked that there is nearly always a little accretion of spongy snow in the centre of hailstones. This is their only opaque portion; the concentric layers that surround it have all the transparency of ordinary ice. The nucleus and its coverings therefore do not seem to be formed in the same manner. Sometimes there fall heavy hailstones with a snowy centre which are composed of rings or layers alternately transparent and opaque. The fine soft hail seen in autumn and winter particularly, the surface of which looks as though powdered with flour, is usually called *sleet*. It is, properly speaking, a kind of middle formation between hail and snow.

Volta relates that one night in the month of August, 1707, he picked up, during a storm that burst over the town of Como, several hailstones that weighed nearly ten ounces. Darwin mentions a tempest on the pampas of South America, where the icy fragments that fell were so heavy as to kill large animals.

We have just spoken of a hailstorm that happened during the night. This is a very rare occurrence, for it is usually during the hottest hours of the day in summer that hail forms. The clouds that contain it seem to have great depth, and are distinguished from other storm-clouds by their ashy color. Their edges have numerous jagged indentations, and circular movements are sometimes remarked in them. Hail usually precedes storms of rain, and sometimes accompanies them; but it scarcely ever follows them, especially when the rains have lasted for any time. In the tropics, hailstorms have been noticed only on the lofty mountains. None falls in the plains. It is more particularly frequent in the temperate zone, and then becomes more and more rare as we advance toward the polar regions.

In most cases, the phenomenon of hail has a local character. It is very frequent at the outlet of the deep valleys of the Alps and upon the lower acclivities that separate them from the plains. The low lands of Borgo-franco, near the Val d'Aosta, are scourged by it every year. At Clermont, at the foot of the Puy-de-Dôme, hail falls very often, while on the heights, half a league distant, but one fall of hail has been recorded in the last twenty-three years! Sometimes there are great storms during which hail falls over a vast extent of territory, but these are fortunately rare.

The formation of hail has been more easily explained since the discovery by aëronauts of very cold atmospheric layers (the thermometer marking 40°) at heights comparatively limited, and that too in midsummer. These layers, as we have already said, are filled with fine needles of ice, which, when packed together, may form the nucleus of the hailstones, upon which the vapors solidify themselves in other layers. The existence of whirlwinds, arising from the collision of opposite currents—chiefly equatorial and polar—explains the suspension and even the ascension, by a spiral movement, of the hailstones that form. Leaves and twigs, torn from trees by a tempest, have been seen to fall at a distance, covered with a coating of ice.

The currents originated by these whirlwinds are generally in opposite electrical conditions before they become mingled. Hence it is remarked that it rarely hails without thunder being heard, and that during such a fall the electricity developed varies not only in degree but in kind.

Some years ago, rows of long poles were planted in the fields in France to serve as *hail-rods*, or protectors against the hail. They were intended to modify the electrical conditions of the atmosphere; but the system was found to fall short of the purpose, and Arago, in arguing against it in one of his learned "Notices," advises farmers to give more of their attention to mutual coöperative associations, until science shall have discovered some better defence against the ravages of the storm.

CHAPTER IV.

PHENOMENA OF THE GLACIERS.

Meteorology of the Glaciers.—Their Formation.—The Grindelwald and Furca Glaciers.—Amphitheatres.—Névés.—Moraines.—Movements of the Glaciers.—Primitive Glaciers.—Polar Glaciers.—Variations of the Seasons and Climate.

METEOROLOGY OF THE GLACIERS.—THEIR FORMATION.

WE have already spoken of the favorable influence of glaciers upon the mean height of the watercourses during each season. In a remarkable note appended to the work on "Meteorology," by Kaemtz, M. Chas. Martins, one of the most learned professors of the day, summarily examines the influence of temperature and aqueous meteors on these solid rivers that, issuing from the region of external snow, descend slowly into the plains, in the midst of forests and cultivated fields.

"If we examine the phenomena presented by the glaciers," says M. Chas. Martins, "in a purely meteorological point of view, we shall see that it is not too rash to maintain that a time will come when we shall be enabled to judge the modifications of the atmosphere by those of the glaciers, and *vice versa*. But in order thus to establish in a positive manner the link that unites the meteorology and the physical exterior of the globe, it is desirable to make a long series of meteorological observations in the vicinity of the glaciers, so as to bring the two kinds of phenomena into direct *rapport*."

Before making known some of the modifications indicated in this passage, we must pause for a brief space to consider the formation of the glaciers. This is the point of departure recommended by M. Martins for the desired observations.

When, in summer, the clouds disperse, after the tempests of rain that fall in the plains, the summits of the mountains are seen whitened with newly-fallen snow, which melts very quickly in the sun, but remains on the highest peaks, in the region of *eternal snows*, as low down as a certain limit that varies according to the country and the exposure. This limit, when traced upon an extended chain of mountains, appears to be almost horizontal; but, at certain points in the depth of the valleys, the glaciers are seen descending in long white trains to the plain. M. George Altmann, in his "Treatise on the Icy Mountains of Switzerland," has given the following description of the Grindelwald glacier, so often explored by naturalists:

THE GRINDELWALD AND FURCA GLACIERS.

"The village of Grindelwald is situated in a long and narrow gorge of the mountains. From that point we begin to get a glimpse of the glacier, but, in order to see it in its full extent, we must go higher up. Then one of the finest spectacles that can be imagined is revealed. It is a sea of ice, or an immense expanse of frozen water, which descends into the valley along the slope of a lofty mountain. From this frozen reservoir starts a prodigious mass of pyramids heaped together, forming a kind of curtain that occupies the whole breadth of the valley, an expanse of about eight hundred yards, and is bordered on both sides by lofty mountains, covered with verdure and a forest of pines up to a certain height. This accumulation of pyramidal forms looks like a sea agitated by the winds, the waves of which have been suddenly congealed by the frost; or, rather, one beholds an amphitheatre formed by an immense assemblage of icy hillocks of a bluish color, and each of them from thirty to forty feet in height. The point of view is of marvellous beauty. Nothing is comparable to it, especially when, in summer, the sun darts its rays upon this group of glittering pyramids. Then the entire glacier begins to smoke, and glows with a brightness that dazzles the eyes."

We will add to this description the account of the Furca glacier given by Coxe in his " Letters on Switzerland":

" After long efforts and a toilsome march over immense stretches of snow and ice that came in our way, with precipices and torrents constantly beneath our feet, we reached the upper part of the valley by an extremely steep ascent. The great number of forked and irregular masses of rock which, accumulated around this valley, stud the summit of the eminence, have, it is said, originated the name now given it of the *Forks* or *Furca*. The region in which we then were, appeared more frightful and desolate than even the most desert parts of Saint Gothard. Below us, it is true, the mountains were clad in rich verdure, and bestrewn with fragrant flowers; but vegetation did not reach to the height where we were. The most savage sterility surrounded us, and near by there rose a fearful accumulation of ice, from which there descended a cataract that, rolling toward the Valais, is no doubt one of the sources of the Rhone. This glacier was on our left and a little above us, and never did any mass of objects, however grand or terrible, present to us a combination of beauty at once so terrifying and so sublime.

"From that point we descended a mass of broken rocks which, in every direction, bristle the ridges of a long line of precipices. I then felt sufficiently fatigued to require rest and refreshment. We seated ourselves on the banks of a very limpid streamlet which flowed briskly down the mountain, the latter being so steep that our little repast had to be propped to prevent it from rolling away from us. Before us the Furca glacier lay extended in all its beauty. It is an immense mass of ice that spreads out, in the form of an amphitheatre, between two heaps of rocks more jagged, if possible, than any that we saw in the neighboring mountains. This amphitheatre entirely fills the precipice that separates them, and rises gradually from their base to a short distance from their summits. The sun, which darted its rays perpendicularly upon the glacier, gave it the brightness and transparency of crystal, while the shadows of its vast fragments, admirably colored, intersected its dazzling whiteness with all the varying tints of a truly celestial blue. Terrible cracking noises, indicative of new crevices forming in the glacier, were heard several times; and the Rhone, pouring along at its feet in the form of a torrent, mingled its continuous roaring with the din. It is in a great measure to the accumulation of ice that I have just described that the river owes its existence."

CIRCLES.—NÉVÉ.—MORAINES.

Ramond, the naturalist, the intrepid explorer of the Alps and Pyrenees, and the translator of Coxe's book, has added to his translation some excellent observations on the glaciers, and has been one of the first to point out a part of the causes that concur in their formation and determine their progress. Before him, Haller, De Saussure, and De Luc, had already established a number of important facts. But it is to more recent researches that we owe the explanation of most of the phenomena connected with the nature and movement of glaciers.

"Snow accumulates around the high peaks in deep depressions known as amphitheatres. It is in descending from these amphitheatres toward the valleys that the snow is transformed, under the influence of the sun and nocturnal frosts, to small grains of transparent ice, and that this granulated mass, called *névé* in Switzerland, becomes converted, by pressure and successive congelations, to a moving mass of ice, sometimes white and filled with bubbles of air, and sometimes more compact and skyey blue."

Such is the origin of the glaciers, which their own weight causes to advance slowly in the direction of the declivities. Huge crevices are produced during this movement, and the water that drips down into them when the snow melts, accelerates it by hollowing out cavities in the lowermost parts of the mass. Besides, when the water thus contained in the glacier dilates by a new congealment, the entire mass increases in volume, and extends in the direction where it finds the least resistance, that is to say, from the higher point to the lower. This continual progression of the glaciers has been proved by incontestable facts.

A bed of pebbles and sand being interposed between the bottom of the glacier and the rock, the result is, that the action of the masses of ice in movement polishes the surface over which they descend, and makes creases and furrows running in the same direction. This effect has been well ascertained, not only in the ice-caverns that are sometimes found at the extremities of the glaciers, but also on the rocks that border them. These rocks, rounded by the ponderous effort of the mass that presses them, often assume a particular aspect, which renders them distinguishable at a distance, wherever a glacier has worn itself a bed. Some of these, seen far away, look like flocks of sheep, and for this resemblance De Saussure the naturalist has invented the term *roches moutonnées*, or "sheep-shaped rocks."

Another order of phenomena demands our attention. As M. Martins has well said, in his "Researches on the Glacier Period," "The Alps are immense ruins. Every thing conspires for their destruction; all the elements seem to have combined to bring down their proud summits. The masses of snow that weigh upon them so heavily in winter, the rain that filters in between their beds in summer, the sudden action of torrents, the less abrupt but still more powerful operation of chemical affinities, wear away, separate, and decompose the hardest rocks. Their *débris* falls from the upper heights, into the amphitheatres occupied by the glaciers, in the form of considerable land-slides, accompanied by a terrific uproar and immense clouds of dust. Even in midsummer I have seen avalanches of stone precipitate themselves from the uppermost summits of the Schreckhorn, and form upon the hitherto spotless snow a long black streak, made up of enormous blocks and a countless number of smaller fragments."

These blocks, some of which measure from ten to twenty yards in thickness, either way, are borne along by the glacier, and consequently form long streaks, which skirt across its borders, or accumulate in transversal lines at its extremities. These streaks of *débris*, left by the avalanches and land-slides, have received the name of *moraines*.

MOVEMENTS OF THE GLACIERS.—PRIMITIVE GLACIERS.

By these interesting observations, not only has the movement of the glaciers been circumstantially proved, but we have been enabled to demonstrate their ancient extent by the furrows grooved in the rock by the primitive glaciers, and by following in the valleys the traces of their lateral and transversal *moraines*.

Thus, the glaciers of Mont Blanc once extended from Chamouni to Geneva. On the eastern slope of Jura there are found isolated bowlders, or *wandering blocks*, so called, of granite, which can have come from no other source than the mountains of Switzerland, the Jura chain being composed of calcareous stone. The immense glacier, which transported these blocks to the height of a thousand yards above the level of the sea, extended across the plain that is comprised between the Alps and the Jura. It was, in Martins's opinion, the principal glacier of Switzerland, the others, which are also indicated by the plainest traces, being but its tributaries.

To Jean Perraudin, a chamois-hunter, the first idea of this cataclysm is due. A learned geologist, M. de Charpentier, to whom he had communicated the result of his observations, made it the subject of persevering research, and obtained the most incontestable proof of the grand phenomenon which had been pointed out to him. The study of the glacier period is thus connected with the revolutions of which our globe has been the theatre. Numerous scientific works, among which we must mention in the first rank those of M. Agassiz, have indicated in the two hemispheres the same traces of antediluvian glaciers, extending over the wide plains that surround our mountain-ranges.

Professor Tyndall, in his fine work on "The Glaciers of the Alps," attributes the present conformation of the Alpine chain, in a great measure, to the movements of those prodigious masses of ice which have traced immense furrows in the rock, hollowed out the valleys to great depths as they passed, and by this very action prepared their partial destruction. In fine, Mr. Tyndall explains that the currents of warm air that rise from the valleys toward the heights, have a temperature the more elevated and a force the greater the deeper the valley is. Hence it results that the glacier grows smaller as it sinks lower, and that it reaches limits at last which it cannot pass. This equilibrium between the thaws of summer and the increase and advance of winter appears to be established at the present day, and, with some rare exceptions, we know the mean limit beyond which the ice never goes.

We find among the Pyrenees, the Vosges, the mountains of Scotland, and the principal ranges on the globe, the same traces of an immense development of primitive glaciers. We are ignorant, as yet, of the cause of this phenomenon, superinduced, as it was, no doubt, by meteorological conditions very different from those now existing, but which persevering observation of the disturbances taking place under our eyes will perhaps enable us to discover. Thus, Professor

Frankland, of the Royal Institution of London, has recently shown that the limit of the eternal snows is higher in the interior of continents than in the vicinity of seas. It may be readily understood, in fact, how an abundant production of watery vapor is one of the principal causes of the formation of glaciers, the vapor becoming snow and ice in the high regions of the atmosphere. But the abundance of aqueous meteors is also in correspondence, as we have seen, with the temperature, so that it is impossible to admit the existence of the immense glaciers of which the traces and deeply-worn channels are found on all sides, at the very period when the mean temperature of the globe was above the present temperature. The chains of mountains, which had just then appeared, had not yet been encroached upon by the slow but potent action of the different agents of destruction that excavate and reduce them, and those primitive chains presented a vast surface for the accumulation of snow and ice, the formation of which was favored by the more frequent vicinity of great lakes and interior seas, such as the ancient sea of Sahara, indicated by Charles Lyell in his "Principles of Geology."

Maury, in his excellent researches on the geological part performed by the winds, has put in the way of completion some important discoveries regarding the relations that subsist between the quantity of moisture set in circulation by the atmosphere and the configuration of the seas and continents. The action of the great aërial currents, as well as that of the great oceanic currents, varies with the circumstances that favor or obstruct it, and these variations are in close relation to the distribution of heat upon the globe. It is to these causes, which are still incessantly at work, that Mr. Lyell attributes also "the principal revolutions of the meteorological condition of the atmosphere at different geological epochs."

The conflict of the elements, subjected, according to the region, to the influence of heat and cold, necessarily produced convulsions corresponding in extent and intensity to the greater or less power of these influences, and left on the surface of the globe the deep traces that science discovers there to-day. "The phenomena," says M. Martins, "have remained the same; but, instead of those gigantic manifestations characteristic of the geological epochs preceding our own, they restrict themselves to the limits of action which have been imposed upon them by the equilibrium of the period of repose that the coming of man has inaugurated on the earth."

POLAR GLACIERS.

The limit of the eternal snows descends lower in passing from the equator to the poles, from the glaciers of the Cordilleras that cover the volcanoes of Peru, to those of Spitzbergen, which come down to the edge of the sea, and fill up the bottom of the bays. These last-mentioned glaciers present a remarkable peculiarity. Upon the western coast of the island, bathed by one of the branches of the great lukewarm current of the Atlantic—the Gulf Stream—the sea thaws during the summer, and melts the lower part of the glaciers, which, continually advancing, at length pass beyond the shore. The parts which are no longer supported below are then seen detaching themselves and forming the field-ice that is met with in such quantities in the Arctic Ocean. Madame Leonie d'Aunet has described this phenomenon, as follows, in her interesting " Voyage to Spitzbergen" :

" During my sleep the thaw had commenced, and the physiognomy of the day had changed as though by a miracle. A spectacle of the utmost turbulence and agitation had succeeded to the motionless solitude of the evening before. A flotilla of islands of ice surrounded the corvette, and covered the bay as far as the eye could see. The ices of the pole, which no dust has ever soiled, as pure now as on the first day of the creation, are tinged with the most vivid colors. One would say the rocks were precious stones. One sees the sparkle of the diamond, and the dazzling hues of the sapphire and the emerald, blended in an unknown and marvellous substance. These floating islets, incessantly undermined by the sea, change their forms at every instant. By an abrupt movement their base becomes their summit; a needle changes to a mushroom; a column imitates an immense table; a tower is transformed to a staircase. And all this is so rapid and unexpected that one cannot help thinking that some supernatural power must control the sudden transformations. At all events, from the first moment, I fancied that I saw before me the ruins of a fairy city suddenly destroyed by a superior power, and condemned to disappear without leaving a single vestige where it had stood. I saw fragments of architecture in every style and of every period dashing together around me—belfries, columns, minarets, ogives, pyramids, turrets, cupolas, crenellated battlements, volutes, arcades, pediments, colossal masses of masonry, carvings as delicate as those that encircle the slender pillars of our cathedrals—all there confounded and commingled in one common disaster. The palette could not reproduce, and mere description cannot convey, an idea of this strange and wondrous combination.

"This place, where every thing is cold and inert, is represented as being wrapped in a profound and gloomy silence, is it not? Well, a totally different conception of it must be formed. Nothing could reproduce the tremendous tumult of a day of thaw at Spitzbergen.

"The sea, studded with sharp pinnacles of ice, plashes noisily; the tall masses bristling along the coast slide down, break from the rest, and plunge into the gulf with a terrific crash; the mountains crack and split apart; the waves dash furiously against the granite capes; the islands of ice as they break up make a succession of crackling sounds like discharges of musketry, and the gust tosses whirling clouds of snow on high with hoarse roarings. It is terrible! It is magnificent! One seems to hear the choirs of the abyss of the old world intoning the prelude to a new chaos."

VARIATIONS OF THE SEASONS AND OF CLIMATES.

We have seen how the melting of the glaciers maintains the volume of the rivers during the summer-time, and thus, in keeping up the watercourses, contributes to refresh and fertilize our fields. The floating ices of the pole, which then descend toward our latitudes, also moderate the heat of our summers by the influence of winds and currents. Sometimes, even, as a learned meteorologist, M. Renou, has remarked, a cold summer like that of 1816 may be the consequence of a great breaking up of the polar ices.

The regions adjacent to the two poles may be considered as immense glaciers, resting upon rocks of greater or less elevation, and sometimes upon lofty mountains, the summits of which pierce the snow. Two volcanoes, the *Erebus* and the *Terror*, were discovered in 1841 by Sir James Ross, during his expedition to the Antarctic regions. The *Erebus*, which is about 12,000 feet in height, and covered with snow to the crater, threw out dense volumes of smoke at intervals.

A knowledge of the causes that, in these regions, determines the periodical increase or diminution of the ice, would be of great interest for the general meteorology of the globe. These variations seem to be connected with a variation of seasons dependent upon the periodicity of the solar spots, as M. Renou indicates, or on the movements of the earth in its orbit, as hinted by

Jean Reynaud, when referring to the secular variation of climates in his "Terre et Ciel." But a long series of observations on the glaciers of both hemispheres would be necessary, in order to solve these important questions with any certainty.

Already numerous discoveries, due to the intrepid zeal, the devotion, and the scientific skill of the great explorers who penetrated the icy solitudes of the pole, and the burning deserts of the equator, or climbed the perilous summits of our highest mountains, have opened new horizons to investigation. In the vast totality of meteoric phenomena, until then so confused, we have, through their aid, seen a few simple laws stand forth that shall hereafter serve to guide us in studying the perturbations of the atmosphere and the modifications that they lead to on the surface of the globe.

CHAPTER V.

THUNDER-STORMS.

Luminous Phenomena.—The Fires of St. Elmo.—Thunder-storms among the Mountains.—The Forms of Lightning.—Globular Thunder-bolts.—Thunder.—Singular Effects of Lightning.—Lightning-rods.—Geography of Thunder-storms.—Influence of the Soil.—Volcanic Storms.—Action of Thunder-storms upon the Subterranean Waters.—Utility of Thunder-storms.

LUMINOUS PHENOMENA.— FIRES OF ST. ELMO.

THE air during a thunder-storm is sometimes so highly charged with electricity, that it becomes visible in the midst of the obscurity by a vivid light resting on all surrounding bodies, and particularly upon the water. Mention is made of luminous rains, during which the ground seemed to be on fire. More than once travellers have been seized with alarm on seeing their wet clothes all aglow on stormy nights. A curious narrative addressed by M. Allemand, a physician of Fleurier, near Neufchâtel, to Professor Piotet, as mentioned in the *Bibliothèque Universelle* of Geneva, sets forth à case of this kind :

"On the third of May last, I was called to Motiers about ten o'clock in the evening, and was surprised, so to speak, as I was leaving the village, by a storm that was quickly followed by a very heavy rain. Although provided with a walking-stick umbrella, I thought I had better close it, as the thunder grew more frequent and severe, and I even held the upper end, which, as you may know, forms a metallic point, in my hand; the point is blunt indeed, yet it might attract the lightning. Ere long, the night, which was excessively dark already, became more so with torrents of rain, and it was only by the help of the vivid and frequent flashes of lightning, that I was able to pursue my way. Thus moving along through the most violent tempest that can be imagined in our part of the country, I suddenly noticed a light that appeared to come from above, and, at once raising my eyes, I remarked that it was the brim of my hat that seemed to be illuminated. Thinking that it was real fire, and without taking time to reflect, I suddenly passed my hand along the luminous edge, expecting to extinguish it. But, to my great surprise, it only shone the brighter, and this gave me a confused idea that I had been mistaken as to the character of the light. My hand was full of water that flowed from my hat, and, in making a motion to shake it off, I saw it shine like a piece of polished metal reflecting a bright light.

"Hereupon, to the sensations that I had experienced until then, succeeded such emotion as caused me to utter half aloud an exclamation of fear. I was then about one hundred paces from the Chaux farm, that is to say, about ten minutes' walk from Fleurier, and fifteen or twenty from Motiers. I deliberated for a moment whether I should seek shelter in the farm-house, or continue on my way; but, at last, some scientific reasoning in my own mind, and profound reliance upon the Supreme Author of the formidable apparatus by which I was surrounded, decided me to push on. Having been enabled to fill my hand unharmed with the electric water that gleamed along the brim of my hat, I felt emboldened to repeat the experiment—although, after all, I did so the second time with a sort of fear — and ascertain whether this phosphorescent light had no odor, and whether it produced neither a crackling sound nor sparkles of flame. But I saw only the beautiful light I had remarked in the first instance, which did not rise from my hand at the moment when I opened it, but seemed to be applied to its surface like a shining varnish. This light lasted only for an instant. Continuing on my way, with my gaze almost constantly riveted upon the brilliant halo that bordered my hat, I saw another vivid light on the surface of the smooth handle of my umbrella, at the spot where the metallic plate is usually found on which the name of the owner is engraved. My first movement was to pass my thumb over the place, in order to extinguish this new fire, which had become as perplexing to me as the other. The same phenomenon ensued; that is to say, the part rubbing became quite as luminous as the part rubbed. I then felt afraid of the umbrella, the metallic mounting of which was continually before my mind, and I threw it down. The thunder-claps increased, although the electric concussion seemed to be, and was, indeed, at some distance from me. Once relieved of my umbrella, I endeavored to rub the rim of my beaver briskly with the sleeve of my coat, but this had no other effect than to make the crown of light more vivid, and I arrived with it at Motiers. I attribute its cessation to the proximity of the tall poplars that border the road near that village."

These effects are explained by the influence of the storm-clouds in the upper region of the atmosphere. The latter attract, at the surface of the soil, an electricity contrary to that with which they are charged. Frequently the pencils of rays that one sees at the extremity of the points placed on an electric machine in operation, appear in enlarged dimensions upon all kinds of salient objects, metallic bars and uprights, the spires of belfries, and the masts and yard-arms of ships. Those brilliant little flames, which sailors call *the fires of St. Elmo*, indicate the abundant emission of the terrestrial fluid, neutralizing the fluid of the clouds. We shall cite, in addition to the above, only the following facts, as Arago gives them:

"On January 14, 1824, just after the close of a storm, M. Maxadorf, happening to look at a wagon loaded with straw, in the middle of a field near Gothen, over which hung a huge black cloud, observed that every stalk stood out straight and seemed on fire. Even the whip of the driver threw off a vivid light. The phenomenon disappeared as soon as the wind had swept away the black cloud, but it had lasted ten minutes.

"On the 8th of May, 1831, after sunset, some officers were walking bareheaded, during a storm, on the terrace of the Bab-Azoun fort in Algiers, when each of the party remarked with surprise, as he looked at his neighbor, that there were little pencils of light at the ends of his hair. When these officers raised their hands, similar luminous plumes formed at the ends of their fingers."

STORMS AMONG THE MOUNTAINS.

A Swiss engineer, M. Buchwalder, was engaged in geodesic operations on the summit of Mont Sentis, at a height of seven thousand five hundred feet above the level of the sea, when he was caught in a violent storm. "Heavy clouds," he says, "coming from the west, enveloped the mountain. Very soon a violent wind announced a tempest; thunder was heard in the distance, and the hail fell in such abundance that, in a few minutes, it covered Mont Sentis with a sheet of ice. We took refuge in our tent, and I carefully closed all the openings so as to leave no hold to the wind. For a few moments, the storm seemed to abate, but it was only an interval of silence, a respite, during which a terrible crisis was in preparation. In fine, at eight o'clock in the morning, the thunder was heard again, but much nearer and more violent, and it continued thus, for hours together, without cessation. Tired of my long imprisonment under the tent, I went outside, to note the condition of the sky and measure the depth of the hail that had fallen. Scarcely had I taken a few steps in the open air, ere the thunder burst over my head with such fury that I deemed it prudent to regain the shelter of my tent, and my aid followed my example. In order to diminish the danger of being struck by the lightning, we lay down side by side upon some planks. At this moment a cloud, as dense and black as night, enveloped Sentis. The rain and hail fell in torrents; the wind blew with fury, and the flashes of lightning succeeded each other incessantly, crossing and recrossing in every direction, and surrounded us with a lurid light like the reflection of a fire. The crashes of thunder, rebounding from the precipitous sides of the mountain, leaped from echo to echo with such vehemence that we could scarcely hear ourselves speak. The sound was a sharp, rending noise; a quivering crash, as though the heavens had fallen in, and a dull prolonged roar, all in one. At length, the fierceness of the storm became so terrible that my companion could not restrain an emotion of alarm, and asked me if we were not in imminent danger of losing our lives. I endeavored to reassure him by mentioning the fact that Arago and Biot, during their observations in Spain, were surprised by a similar tempest. The lightning had struck their tent, but had glanced off from the cloth without hurting them.

"Hardly had I told him this, ere I heard a cry of distress: 'O my God!'—and at the same instant I saw a ball of fire flash from the feet to the head of my companion, and felt a violent shock in my left leg. Our tent, also, was torn asunder in the middle with a terrific detonation. I turned toward my companion; the unfortunate man had been struck by the thunder-bolt! In the light yielded by the tearing open of the tent, I saw the left side of his face dotted with red and brown spots caused by the electric fluid. His hair, his eyelashes, and his eyebrows, were singed and burnt; his lips and nostrils were a livid blue; his breast heaved for a moment, and then the sound of his breathing ceased. I was suffering horribly myself; but, forgetting my own mishap in my anxiety to aid my companion, who, I saw, was dying, I called him aloud, I shook him, but he made no response. His right eye, which was wide open, brilliant and full of intelligent meaning, seemed turned upon me to implore my assistance, but the left eye remained closed, and, on parting the lids, I saw that it was dull and leaden. I still thought that there was a remnant of life in him, but only for a moment; three times I tried to close that right eye, which was still gazing fixedly at me, and three times it opened again, with all the look of life. I then placed my hand over his heart; it no longer beat. At last, my grief put an end to this distressing examination. My own left leg was paralyzed, and I felt an acutely painful shivering in it, accompanied by an extraordinary agitation or *boiling* of the blood. A convulsive tremor ran through my whole body; a general stifling sensation half choked me, and my heart beat in the most tumultuously irregular manner. Was I to perish like my hapless companion? Thank God, however, I managed to reach the nearest village, after extreme exertion. Subsequently I discovered that my instruments had been struck by the lightning, for every metallic article that the tent contained when the thunderbolt fell, bore traces of the passage of the fluid. The points, edges, and most delicate parts, were softened and melted."

THE FORMS OF LIGHTNING.—GLOBULAR LIGHTNING.

Sometimes the clouds, during a storm, seem to give out a continual emission of electricity, for they remain luminous a long time, as Rozier, the physiologist, observed, during a storm of great intensity that he witnessed in the environs of

Beziers. "Little by little," he says, "a luminous point that made its appearance in the midst of dense clouds, assumed breadth and volume. It then, by imperceptible degrees, formed a zone, or phosphorescent band, which revealed itself to my eyes as about three feet in height; it at last subtended an angle of sixty degrees. Above this first zone, another formed of about the same height, but of not more than thirty degrees' measurement. An open space of about the same extent separated them. In both these belts were noticed irregularities similar to those seen on the edges of the heavy clouds that are the forerunners of a storm. These edges were not equally luminous, although the centre of the belts presented a uniform brightness. While they were advancing toward the east, the lightning darted three different times from the end of the lower belt, but without any appreciable detonation." This phenomenon lasted for a quarter of an hour, and was dispelled by a violent gust from the southward, that carried the storm to a distance.

These intermittent discharges of electricity have very varied forms, and traverse the atmosphere with astonishing velocity. Wheatstone has demonstrated that the most brilliant and extended lightnings—sometimes from fifteen to eighteen miles in length—do not last the thousandth part of a second. Some consist of very delicate shafts of light, with very sharply-defined borders, describing zigzag lines in space, and sometimes dividing into several branches. Most usually they are white, and sometimes, but rarely, purplish, violet-hued, or bluish.

Others extend, on the contrary, over a wide surface, and have neither the whiteness nor the brilliant illumination of those before mentioned. Their hue is often a very vivid red. "These lightnings," says Arago, "appear, sometimes, to illuminate only the outlines of the clouds from which they emanate. Sometimes, too, their vivid light embraces the entire superficial extent of those same clouds, and, moreover, seems to issue from the interior of them. One might say with truth that the clouds open. Such is the popular expression, and I should search in vain for others to depict the same phenomenon more accurately."

The first kind of lightning is much more rare than the second. In ordinary storms, hundreds of the latter appear for every one instance of linear, or, more especially, of forked lighting. We will here quote the description of a remarkable storm observed by M. Liais during his sojourn in Brazil.

Although it was the 30th of January, the thermometer marked thirty-three degrees. "During the night, the wind came up very feebly from the southwest; in the morning the air was pure, and a burning sun fell upon the soil, still damp with the rain of the preceding days. In the afternoon there were seen some cirri. Toward evening other clouds, cumulus and cumulo-stratus formed, and, at sunset, the sky was almost covered.

"At seven o'clock, flashes of lightning were seen in the east, and, at ten minutes past seven, the storm had acquired all its intensity. At that time, zigzag lightnings were darting forth continually, at least one-third of them forked. These flashes were white, and very vivid. Sometimes, they seemed to tend slightly toward a bluish tinge, and, at others, were of an orange hue. They did not form interrupted zigzags, as they do in many storms, but rather broken lines, and, moreover, each of these lines was sinuous. These lightnings did not end in points, but generally presented a slightly-rounded form at the extremity where they terminated. Although these flashes had great velocity, it seemed to me that their development, and the manner of their propagation, could be followed with greater facility than in ordinary storms. Two flashes were very rarely seen at the same time, and their emission had a certain regularity.

"The most of these flashes were unaccompanied by any noise. From time to time we could hear a slight rumbling in the distance, but, owing to its frequency, without being able to distinguish to what flash it belonged. Many of them seemed to issue from a sort of very small cumulus, situated but a little distance above the horizon, and to propagate themselves with an apparent ascensional movement. Others seemed to issue from the upper bed of clouds, with an apparent inverse movement. The storm was not accompanied by rain. Only at the beginning a few large drops had fallen. The upper cloud, upon which the lightnings shot out in relief, did not cover the entire face of the sky, and a few stars could be seen.

"I pass on now to the most singular part of the phenomenon. Besides the two-forked lightnings and those with three or four offshoots, which were also very frequent, not a moment went by without our seeing also what might be termed *arborescent* or tree-shaped lightning. These were flashes that divided themselves into several principal branches, which in their turn split off into a multitude of smaller boughs, that again presented the same sinuosities, and the same rounded endings noticed in the other flashes. There was no other means of counting these branches than by reproducing immediately on paper the impression made on the retina of the eye. One of these flashes, that I had remarked particularly, and that had appeared to propagate itself as it descended, divided, at first into two branches, which subdivided in their turn, in such manner as to form fifteen branches in all. Another was of radiating form, and one arborescent, that is to say, its propagation was in every direction, but starting from a common centre.

"The tempest seemed to continue motionless. At the end of about ten minutes, the frequency of the flashes diminished; at a quarter past eight, they ceased, and the clouds soon dispersed. The zodiacal light was seen in the west and the east, below the milky way, spanning the entire sky. It may be well to mention that on the preceding evening the phosphorescence of the sea was extraordinary, and such as I had never seen it before. On the evening of the storm, on the contrary, it had resumed its usual appearance under the tropics."

In another storm, M. Liais again noticed the extremely curving shape of the ends of the arborescent flashes, and a still more marked tendency to terminate in balls of fire. Three times these balls broke off, leaving a train of light behind them, like a *bolide*, and traversing an arc on the sky of thirteen degrees in half a second. We have seen the origin of a third kind of lightning, which the physiologists call *globular lightning*, without being able, up to the present time, either to explain it or to imitate it, as they do with ordinary lightning. It is entirely analogous, excepting in dimensions, to the sparks of an electric battery. These globes of fire, which are sometimes as large as a bomb, descend to the ground with a motion slow enough to enable the observer to note their shape. Their color varies from dead white to vivid red. In advancing along the soil, they seem to keep aloof from the surface of objects and emit no heat. They are sometimes seen to stop for an instant, then to advance again, and then rebound, like an elastic ball, or divide into several smaller globes. Sometimes, at the end of their course, a plume seems to issue from them, and then they explode with a noise like that of a cannon, hurling zigzag lightnings on all sides of them, that produce the most fearful ravages.

THUNDER.—SINGULAR EFFECTS OF LIGHTNING-STROKE.

The sound caused by a single flash of lightning sometimes lasts without interruption as much as forty-five seconds. Although it is true that all the beds of air lying along the course of the immense electric spark are shaken, so to speak, at the same time, the sound developed at each point reaches the observer only by successive concussions, and the difference in distance produces the variations noticed in the violence of the thunder, its rolling reverberations, and its sudden crashes, repeated again and again by the echoes. The discharges that take place between a cloud and any terrestrial object are the most severe.

We cannot account for some of the phenomena of transporting power revealed by lightning, unless we call in some other force than electricity. It was beyond all doubt the power of steam alone, eliminated on its passage, which could, for instance, lift a wall weighing twenty-six tons, and carry it in one mass a distance of many yards. Repeatedly, the roofs of huge edifices have been swept off as though by the explosion of a mine.

In passing through bodies, the lightning very rapidly raises their temperature. Metallic conductors nearly a third of an inch thick have been melted by it, and, when of less dimensions, have been completely volatilized. Bell-wires are found incrusted in tiny drops in the floor, or shot in fine dust over the walls.

Travellers often see the surface-beds of rock on the tops of mountains vitrified by the lightning. When it penetrates beds of sand it forms tubes of melted and adhering quartz, sometimes thirty and forty feet in length, which have received the name of *fulgurites*. The following fact is cited by M. Jamin: " On the 17th of July, 1823, the lightning struck a birch-tree, near the village of Rauschen, on the borders of the Baltic. The inhabitants, who hurried to the spot, saw two deep, narrow holes close to the tree, and one of them seemed warm to the touch, notwithstanding the rain. Professor Hagen, of Koenigsberg, caused the ground around the holes to be dug away with great care. The warm one presented nothing peculiar; the other also, for the depth of a foot or so, offered nothing remarkable, but a little lower down commenced a vitrified tube. The fragility of the tube, however, did not admit of its being taken out in pieces over an inch or two in length. The inside glassy lining was very shiny, of a pearl-gray color, and studded with black points along its entire extent."

Masses of iron and steel traversed by lightning become magnetic, and numerous observations show that, on board of vessels that have been struck, the compasses have been made to deviate from their normal direction. Trees, which are excellent conductors, because of their moisture, are often struck. In such cases, where the burning of the tree has not ensued, the trunk is seen to be dried up and divided into long strips. Inside of houses, all combustible bodies take fire on the passage of lightning through them.

LIGHTNING-RODS.

The identity of electricity and lightning was proved by Franklin. " In order to verify a conjecture he had formed on the subject," says Mignet, one of his biographers, "he undertook to draw electric fluid from the clouds. The first means that occurred to him was to erect pointed iron rods that might attract it This device not seeming practical to him, upon mature reflection, because he could not find any place sufficiently high, he conceived another. He constructed a kite of two pieces of stick, covered with a silk handkerchief. The longer stick he terminated with an iron point at its upper extremity. He then tied to the kite a hempen cord ending with a silk one. Where the hempen cord, which was a conductor, and the silken one, which was not, joined, he fastened a key, so that the electricity might accumulate there and throw off sparks announcing its presence. With his apparatus thus prepared, Franklin went out to the fields one day during a storm. His kite, carefully secured by its string, which was in its turn made fast to the silk cord, was given to the air, while Franklin himself stood aloof and watched it with anxiety. For some time he saw nothing, and was afraid that he had been mistaken; but, all at once, the string at both ends stiffened and the key became charged. It was the electricity descending. Franklin hastened to the spot where he had secured the string at the lower end, presented his finger to the key, and received a smart shock that might have killed him, but, as it was, only filled him with delight."

By the invention of the lightning-rod, Franklin proposed to neutralize the effects of thunder-clouds by furnishing them with an electricity the opposite of their own. He protected buildings with long metallic rods, terminating in sharp points at the top, and communicating with the ground. Along these the terrestrial electricity escapes toward the overhanging cloud, and neutralizes it more or less rapidly. Sometimes, during the night, tall plumes of electric light are seen shining on these points. It may happen that the cloud is not sufficiently discharged, and the lightning may strike between it and the edifice. However, in that case, it falls upon the stem of the rod, which is connected with the ground by an isolated conductor.

The efficacy of lightning-rods is fully demonstrated by statistics. Mr. Snow Harris reports, for instance, that in Devonshire six churches with tall steeples having been struck, one of them only, that was protected by a lightning-rod, suffered no damage. The Church of St. Mark at Venice, the Valentino palace at Turin, the tower of Sienna, all in cities where the lightning causes frequent damage, have likewise been preserved by lightning-rods.

We well remember the terrible thunder-storm that burst over the city of Strasburg on the 14th of August, 1833, about four o'clock in the afternoon. The tower of the cathedral was struck three times in the space of a quarter of an hour. At the last stroke, the whole pile appeared to be in flames for some seconds. In many places, the lead, the copper, the iron, and even the mortar were found to be melted, or vitrified. Fragments of metal had soldered themselves to the bells, and it was found difficult to detach them. Very large masses of stone fell in the neighboring streets. In the next year, one of the turrets was cut in two by the lightning, and it was at last decided to put up lightning-rods on the spire and other parts of the edifice. Since that time, it has been remarked, as a matter of fact, that it has been struck by harmless discharges only, which fell on the rods and followed the conductors into the ground, without the least deviation. Moreover, thunder-storms appear to have become less frequent and less intense over Strasburg.

Let us, also, mention the following instance, where, as Arago phrases it, "Nature was caught in the act." "On the 21st of May, 1831, during a very violent thunder-storm, the ship Caledonia was under sail in Plymouth Bay. From the town, the lightning could be seen darting toward the water, at but a short distance from the vessel. It fell also on the shore and there caused several accidents. Surrounded, as it were, by these falling thunder-bolts, the Caledonia, protected by her lightning-rods, yet escaped all harm and sailed along as safely as though the sky had been clear."

Extreme care, as recommended by all our learned associations, but too often neglected, is required in the construction and keeping of the lightning-rod. It is of special importance that the point should be of metal that will not oxidize, and that the conductor should be united with iron ligatures to all the large metallic pieces of the structure, and be in perfect communication with the ground. In damp soil, the electric flow and dispersion are very easy, but the iron rusts and is quickly worn out. In a dry soil, there would be insulation, and great mishaps might be apprehended. The conductor in such a case must be made to run into a pit full of slacked cinders; coal, when it has been red heated, being an excellent conductor, while it has the additional good property of not attacking iron. When there is a natural sheet of water in the vicinity, the conductor might be led into it, and provided with numerous branching pieces where it does so. A reservoir or cistern cannot be considered in the same light as a well or pit, properly speaking, since the stone blocks and the cement that line its bottom and sides yield but difficult passage to electricity; there is no free dispersion, and a violent concussion might ensue.

The difference in the conducting power of different soils, and of the bodies placed there, should, as well as their form, direct the choice of localities in which one is the least exposed to be struck by lightning. According to the considerations presented in the foregoing pages, care must be taken not to get under trees, or to go too near to large metallic masses, or very high buildings.

Men and animals have been killed beneath a thunder-cloud, without being struck directly by lightning. This phenomenon, called the *return-stroke* by physiologists, is explained by the influence of a very extensive electrified cloud, discharged at one of its extremities by lightning. If, at that moment, then, bodies, beneath the other extremity being powerfully influenced, return suddenly to their natural condition, they experience a very violent shock.

THE GEOGRAPHY OF THUNDER-STORMS.

Humboldt found vitrified surfaces, caused by lightning, on the summit of the mountain of Toluca, at the height of 13,860 feet above the level of the sea. This fact does not prove that thunder-clouds can attain that elevation, for there are cases on record where lightning has struck the tops of mountains, starting from their base. On the other hand, again, the inhabitants of Chamouni affirm that thunder-storms have passed over the summit of Mont Blanc, which is 14,430 feet high.

Arago gives 228, and even 91 feet as the lowermost limit, which, according to exact measurement, can be assigned to thunder-storms.

The principal elements in the geographical distribution of thunder-storms are in relation with the distribution of rain. Nearly all the rain of the tropical regions falls from thunder-clouds, and under the equatorial belt one hears the rumbling of thunder almost continuously. At Calcutta sixty thunder-storms per annum are counted, and among them forty-five occur during the southwest monsoon, that is to say, from April to September. There are none from November to January, or during the northeast monsoon. We have already referred to the exceptional case of Peru, where the inhabitants have never heard thunder.

In the zone of tropical calms, thunder-storms are frequent; less so, however, than under the equator. The example of Europe may give an idea of the state of things in the middle latitudes. In southern Spain there are the same number of thunder-storms, say, from five to ten, as in England and Scandinavia. Italy, the Adriatic Sea, and Greece, present the maximum of the European ratio of thunder-storms. Janina and Rome have forty-five and forty respectively per annum. Among the Alps about thirty are counted. In

France and Germany there are from fifteen to twenty. In the latter country, however, certain localities, such as Munster, Braunsberg, etc., which are exposed to frequent thunder-storms, are remarkable exceptions to this rule.. It is in the Adriatic, and upon the western coasts of Europe, that the winter thunder-storms are most frequent. As we advance toward the east, they become less numerous, and, beyond the frontiers of Germany, only summer thunder-storms are noticed.

In the high latitudes, thunder-storms are extremely rare. Sometimes as long a period as six years will pass without thunder being heard in Greenland. Farther on we shall state how the thunder-storm is replaced in those regions by the splendid phenomena of the aurora borealis.

In the tropics, thunder-storms are always caused by ascending atmospheric currents, and the same is the case with the summer thunder-storms of the temperate zones. They take place every afternoon, when the arrangement of the country is favorable to them. Above some of the lakes of Switzerland there thus daily appears a small cloud that moves over and fixes itself on the slope of a neighboring mountain, and then bursts with a terrific concussion. We have noticed this periodical formation of thunder-storms, toward the close of summer, in the bays of Naples and Tunis.

The thunder-storms of the temperate zone usually accompany the heavy rains that result from the meeting of the equatorial and the polar currents. There then ensues a struggle between the two winds that often lasts for several days, and the result of which determines the state of the weather. With the south winds, the air becomes heavy, warm, and damp, and dense clouds ascend along the horizon. But suddenly the northern gust sweeps down, accompanied with electric explosions. The fluctuations of these currents occasion several consecutive thunder-storms, which exhibit no periodicity, and are of very variable duration. Should the polar wind prevail, all the vapors dissolve in rain, or are borne off to a distance, and the sky clears up again. Upon other occasions, it is the north wind that rules at the outset, with clear, dry, and cold weather, which the arrival of the south wind changes. This current is indicated in the high latitudes by the *cirrus*, which rapidly grows more dense, changes to *cumulus*, and covers the sky with a thick veil of clouds, whence the lightning soon begins to play. When the north wind yields, the thunder-storm winds up with mild weather and those long rains that are so powerful a source of fertility in the temperate zones.

INFLUENCE OF THE SOIL.—VOLCANIC THUNDER-STORMS.

According to some meteorologists, the nature of the ground may contribute to the frequency of thunder-storms. "In the department of Mayenne" (in France), says M. Blavier, a mining-engineer, "there exist masses of *diorite* (a species of rock in which loadstone is sometimes found), which contain a notable proportion of iron, and affect the needle of the compass. We were assured that in certain parishes, such as Niort, for instance, the most threatening thunder-clouds would be seen to disperse as they drew near, or to turn aside in certain directions. We think that the conducting force of several considerable masses of diorite will explain this phenomenon." The savant Vicat reports the following observation, made at Grondone, a village situated among the Apennines, near a very rich iron-mine, that rises in the form of an isolated peak. "Nearly every day, in the months of July and August, an electric cloud is seen forming above this region. The cloud, growing larger by insensible degrees, remains for some hours suspended over the mine,

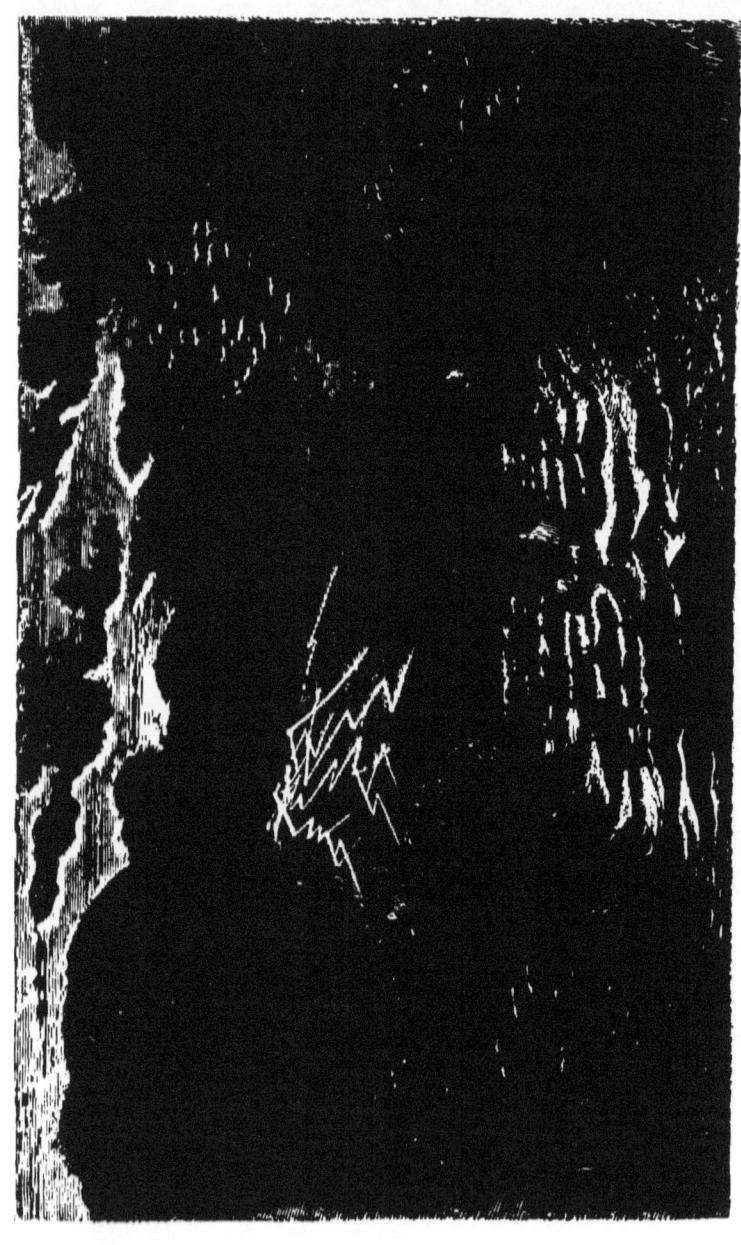

THE LYSE-FIORD

and then, in bursting, discharges itself toward the peak, which is almost entirely metallic. The miners," adds Vicat, "instructed by experience, judge when it is time to quit the spot. They, at the right moment, retire some distance, and then return to their work after the explosion. I have frequently seen the great cloud of Grondone form about noon, and keep together until four or five o'clock, and then, after a few claps, give way to a small thunder-storm."

We find the following curious passage in a recent description of the caves and grottoes of Norway: "A promontory of the Lyse-Fiord contains a cavern really terrible, on account of the meteorological phenomena of which it is the scene. It is well known that there are no rocky cliffs of more sinister aspect than those of the Lyse-Fiord. It is toward the fifty-ninth degree of latitude, at a short distance to the eastward of the port of Stavanger, that this arm of the sea opens. It is a prodigious ditch, twenty-five miles or so in length, shut in between two walls of sharp-pointed, perpendicular rocks of the average height of more than half a mile. No doubt the first mariner who navigated the still, black waters of this chasm, must have proceeded with a certain feeling of horror, asking himself at every turn if he was not about to see some frightful old Norse deity start up before him. Even now it is not without a shudder that one penetrates this sea-defile, in which the ancients would have recognized the entrance to Hades.

"When the southwest wind blows rudely, and plunges by violent gusts into the vast chasm of the Lyse-Fiord, a strange meteoric phenomenon adds to the terrible majesty of the scene. Fifteen hundred feet above the level of the sea, and at two-thirds of the height of the wall that rises to the southward of the entrance to the gulf, there is seen a flash of lightning leaping, from time to time, from the black rock, spreading, then contracting, then expanding, and shrinking again, and dispersing in luminous fringes before it reaches the northern wall. This broad tongue of fire advances, whirling round and round as it goes, and it is to this rotary movement that the apparent expansions and contractions of the lightning are due. Rapid detonations are heard with an increasing power before the live flame leaps from the rock; a violent clap of thunder accompanies it, and reverberates in prolonged echoes through this narrow corridor of the sea. One would think that some battery, hidden behind the cliff, was cannonading some invisible casemate in the opposite wall."

A VOLCANIC STORM.

During volcanic eruptions, the clouds that issue from the craters emit numerous flashes of lightning. These clouds are composed of smoke and vapor, mingled with ashes, and often of ashes alone. In 1631, an immense column of smoke rose from Vesuvius, and was borne for a distance of more than one hundred and twenty miles. During its passage it threw off shafts of lightning, accompanied with thunder, that killed several persons. In another eruption, the cloud, which was extremely black and composed of impalpable ashes, got as far as the town of Tarentum, where the lightning set fire to a number of buildings. These volcanic thunder-storms have also taken place at sea. In 1811, when the island of Sabrina emerged from the waters in the vicinity of the Azores, the columns of dust and ashes that rose from it were furrowed with lightning of extraordinary vividness, according to the statement of the ship-captain who witnessed the phenomenon.

THE EFFECT OF THUNDER-STORMS ON SUBTERRANEAN WATERS.

Arago speaks of modifications that have sometimes taken place in underground waters during stormy weather, in which thunder and lightning play a part; of springs that become troubled and overflow, even after a great drought; of deep wells heard boiling and bubbling noisily; of fountains leaping from the rock with sensibly augmented projectile force. Vallisneri has remarked that the *salsae* and *solfatarae*, or volcanic salt and sulphur fields, in the vicinity of Modena, announce thunder-storms by a sort of ebullition, and by noises resembling thunder.

"Historians and meteorologists," says Arago, "mention local inundations the effects of which seemed to go far beyond what the small quantity of rain issuing from the clouds, and falling within a certain radius, could have led any one to fear." It has rarely happened that, upon such occasions, immense masses of water have not been seen rising from the bowels of the earth, for a greater or less period of time, from openings until then unknown, or that a violent thunder-storm has not been the precursor of the phenomenon and probably its most immediate cause. Such, for instance, were in every particular the circumstances of the inundation that in July, 1688, almost utterly destroyed the villages of Kettlevel and Starbottom in Yorkshire, England. During the storm an immense chasm formed in the adjaccent mountain, and, according to eye-witnesses, the mass of water that gushed from it contributed, as much as the rain, to the ravages that ensued.

In October, 1755, according to Beccaria, a sudden inundation produced great destruction in most of the valleys of Piedmont. The river Po overflowed, and the disaster was preceded by horrible thunder, *orrendi tuoni*, says the learned Italian. Everybody agreed that the principal cause of the inundation was the immense volume of water which, during the storm, suddenly issued through new openings from underground among the mountains.

These local fractures of the solid crust of the globe would have nothing very extraordinary about them, were it proven that, in stormy weather, the water has a tendency to seek the clouds, and that this tendency manifests itself by abrupt outbursts from below. This is precisely the conclusion to be drawn from observations made on board the packet-ship New York in 1827. While the storm raged around the vessel in question, the sea was in a continual ebullition of such a nature as to convey the idea of subterranean volcanoes. Especial note was taken of " three columns of water which leaped high into the air, then fell back, then leaped up again, and once more subsided,"

7

THE USEFULNESS OF THUNDER-STORMS.

Science teaches us to appreciate the beneficent effects of the thunder-storm, the appearance of which was once considered a sign of celestial displeasure. The explosions of thunder and lightning produce a profound modification in the constituent elements of the atmosphere. The gases, which are held merely in a state of simple mixture in the absence of the electric spark, are combined by its agency in such manner as to form new substances, that are detected in various quantities in rain-water. Under certain circumstances these new combinations deposit the nitre that is found on the surface of the soil in different countries. The agricultural efficacy of that substance has been known since the days of antiquity. Virgil mentions it in his "Georgics." Agricultural writers recognize the value of other products of the thunder-storm in helping vegetation. Each electric discharge engenders in the atmosphere fruitful principles of life, which are drawn into the soil, where the roots of plants imbibe them, and so communicate a fresh glow to their foliage and flowers.

Thunder-storms, also, purify the atmosphere. The passage of the lightning gives oxygen more active properties, and transforms it into *ozone*. Although this gas is but little known, we are safe in attributing to it a very energetic agency in destroying miasma and neutralizing putridities that, in spreading throughout the atmosphere, render it unfit for respiration, and give rise to the severest maladies. Ozone may be produced in the laboratory by means of strong electric sparks. If a bell glass be filled with it, spoiled meat and offensive dirt placed under it soon lose their repulsive odor. All the imperceptible remains of organic substances are consumed on coming into contact with the electrified air, and M. Schoenbein has established the fact that air, containing a very small proportion of ozone, will disinfect an equal volume of vitiated atmosphere.

According to recent researches, the hygienic conditions of several regions appear to be in relation to the quantity of ozone in the atmosphere. In many observatories, this quantity is daily ascertained by means of the variations of color revealed by a chemical substance. It is probable that important laws will ultimately be developed from a larger collection of facts.

After a thunder-storm, a peculiar odor, usually spoken of as a *smell of sulphur*, or brimstone, is diffused through the atmosphere. This smell is due to the presence of ozone, and, farther on, we shall see how it manifests itself in the haunts of the great electric meteors that serve the purpose of thunder-storms in the polar regions.

CHAPTER VI.

WHIRLWINDS.

Water-spouts.—Electric Whirlwinds.—Sand-storms.—Water-spouts at Sea.—Water-spouts on Land.—Tornadoes.—Cyclones.—Hurricanes.

WATER-SPOUTS.

"Among the great meteors that come to trouble the apparent order and harmony of Nature—among the grand phenomena which carry terror and desolation wherever they appear, there is one which distinguishes itself from the rest by the strange and gigantic forms it assumes, by the outside forces that it seems to obey, by the unknown and apparently contradictory laws that appear to regulate it, and, to sum up, by the disasters it occasions. These disasters themselves are accompanied by peculiar circumstances, so remarkable that the cause of them cannot be confounded with that of other meteors baleful to humanity. This meteor, so extraordinary, so menacing, and fortunately so rare in our latitudes, is the one designated by the general expression of *water-spout.*"

Such are the words of M. A. Peltier, in his "Observations and Experimental Researches on the Causes that concur in the Formation of Water-spouts."

The least violent and least dangerous whirlwinds are those that are produced by the meeting of contrary winds, and have no other cause than the mechanical impulsion of the forces set in motion during great atmospheric disturbances. Such whirlwinds often form in mountainous countries, where the wind buries itself in the gorges, blows in varying directions, and is sometimes abruptly interrupted by obstacles that turn it aside.

"I have often witnessed these phenomena in the Alps," says Kaemtz, "but will content myself with relating the following fact: A very strong south wind was blowing over the summit of the Righi, and the clouds that passed above my head were sweeping in the same direction. The north wind was blowing toward Zurich, and ascending along the northern slope of the mountain. When it reached the summit, light vapors formed and seemed to seek a passage over the crest, but, the south wind throwing them back, they ascended toward the north, at an angle of forty-five degrees, and disappeared at the top. The struggle of these two contrary winds lasted several hours. A great number of whirlwinds formed at the point where the two winds met, and travellers, who usually feel but little interest in meteoric phenomena, were struck by this singular spectacle."

The terrible whirlwinds that are met with chiefly in the tropics, or accompany great thunderstorms, often spring up in the midst of a calm, and are probably produced by the most formidable forces of electricity. The clouds, according to Peltier, are the source of this power, when, after a rapid evaporation in calm, warm weather, they have retained the electricity that was in the vapors, and that, most usually, is dispersed through the damp atmosphere into the soil. When the clouds, thus charged with electric fluid, and often accumulated in enormous masses, chance to combine their forces with the perturbations of the atmosphere, they act with those that are peculiar to them, and add powerful influences of attraction and repulsion to the violent shocks of the air. All the observations that have been made relative to water-spouts, tend to prove that they are the result of a transformation of these electric clouds.

Before the appearance of these water-spouts,

which are much more frequent at sea than upon the land, black, stormy clouds collect, and the lowermost one in the series is seen descending in the shape of a reversed cone, the point of which approaches the ground or the water in a greater or less degree. Beneath this descending cloud, the waters appear to be in a state of ebullition, and the vapor that issues from them rises like smoke. On land, light bodies, such as dust, etc., are carried upward and form whirlwinds. Sometimes the point of the cone touches the sea, and there hollows out a grand circular depression, as though a violent current of air issued from it. Less frequently, the waters are lifted up in the form of a column, or an ascending cone. In the midst of the vapor-clouds that surround the lower part of the water-spout, sheaves of water gush upward, and fall again on the outside. "This mass of water," says Peltier, "raised in the form of a whirling, boiling smoke; these ascending and descending jets, seen from a distance, have the appearance of a thicket, or a hedge, such as English navigators are accustomed to call 'the bush.'"

Water-spouts nearly always emit a deafening noise, a strange, whizzing sound, which increases or diminishes according to the greater or less dampness of the ground over which they pass.

They are frequently accompanied by whirlwinds in the air, lightning, thunder, hail, and rain.

ELECTRICAL WHIRLWINDS.—SAND-STORMS.

There have been dry, whirling storms, or whirlwinds, that have caused great destruction, without having been preceded by any gathering of opaque clouds. Peltier admits that the invisible vapors collect in transparent clouds that may be charged with electricity, like opaque clouds, and reproduce the same phenomena.

On the great deserts, during a dead calm, and under a blazing sun, the sand sometimes rises in the midst of electric whirlwinds, that remind one of a water-spout. Piddington, in his "Law of Storms," relates a very interesting summary of observations made in Hindostan by Dr. P. Baddely:

"My observations extended from the warm season of 1847, the period of my first coming to Lahore, until 1850; here is the result:

"Sand-storms are caused by spiral columns of electric fluid passing from the atmosphere to the ground. They have a forward movement, a rotary movement, like the whirling storms at sea, and a special spiral movement from top to bottom. It is probable that in an extensive sand-storm, most of these columns move together in the same direction, and that, while the tempest lasts, sudden and numerous gusts take place at intervals, in which the electric tension is at its maximum.

"The same phenomena are to be seen in every case of sand-storm; from those that are but a few inches in diameter, to those that have fifty miles and more of extent, the phenomena are identical.

"It is a curious fact that some of the smallest sand-storms that are seen occasionally in the great arid plains of this country (India) and Afghanistan, above the Bolan Pass, and which are called 'devils' in vulgar parlance, are stationary for a while, that is to say, for an hour or more, and, during all this time, the sand, or dust, and other light bodies from the ground, keep up their whirling movement in the air. In other cases, small sand-storms advance slowly, and when they are numerous they move usually in the same direction. Frequently, birds, such as kites and vultures, soar above these heights, and evidently follow the direction of the column, as though it gave them pleasure. I think that the phenomena associated with sand-storms are identical with those that are presented by water-spouts, in white squalls at sea, and in tornadoes of every description; and that they arise from the same cause, that is to say, from movable columns of electricity.

"In 1847, at Lahore, desirous of satisfying my mind in regard to the nature of sand-storms, I placed in the open air, on the roof of my house, a copper wire insulated upon a bamboo. I led one end of the wire into my room, and put it in communication with an electrometer with a golden plate and a wire connecting with the ground. A day or two afterward, during the passage of a small sand-storm, I had the pleasure of seeing the electric fluid passing from one wire to the other in vivid sparks, and powerfully affecting the electrometer. The fact was, henceforth, explained; and since that time I have, by the same means, taken note of at least sixty sand-storms of different dimensions. All of them presented the same phenomena.

"I have observed that, usually, toward the termination of a storm of this kind, the rain falls suddenly, and that, instantaneously, the current of electricity ceases or greatly diminishes; when it continues, it would seem that it does so only in cases where the storm is of considerable power, and lasts for some time afterward."

The author then gives an account of his method of observing these phenomena, and afterward goes on with his description of whirlwinds:

"The sky is clear; not a breath of air is stirring; but see, presently there is a bank of clouds far down the horizon, and you are surprised that you did not notice them before: a few seconds go by, and the mass of cloud has covered half the celestial hemisphere; there is no time to lose; it is a sand-storm, and every one rushes hurriedly in-doors to escape being caught in it.

"The electric fluid continues to descend incessantly along the conducting wire, while the storm lasts. The sparks are often more than an inch in length, and emit a dull, crackling sound. Its intensity varies with the force of the storm, and, as I said above, is strongest during the sudden gusts.

"One of these storms, which took place last year in the month of August, seemed to come from the direction of Lica, on the Indus, to the west of Lahore. An officer on the march, twenty miles distant from Lica, was suddenly enveloped in it. His tent was swept away, and he was thrown down and nearly suffocated by the sand. At Lica the whirlwind cracked the walls of a solid brick building, in which the same officer had recently lodged, and tore up some trees in the environs by the roots.

"I have repeatedly tried to discover the kind of electricity developed, and have found that it is not invariably the same. Sometimes it appears to be positive, and at others negative. It changes during the storms."

WATER-SPOUTS AT SEA.

The extraordinary effects produced by these tornadoes, their strange destructive power, and the singularity of their forms, prepare our minds to comprehend how they were regarded in old times as evil spirits, who, in this prodigious disguise, rejoiced in desolating the face of the country and spreading terror far and near. Superstition, even now, sometimes attributes a sort of personality to these destructive meteors, whose monstrous aspect and capricious movements vividly strike the imagination. Then the latter, by the aid of ignorance, may give birth to the most absurd fantasies, happily dispelled in our time with ease, by the light of science and reason.

Peltier has reproduced the following account of a whirlwind seen by Dr. Leymerie on the 2d of September, 1804, on board the *Le Vautour:*

"This vessel was coming from Cayenne, steering for the coast of Africa, and was not far from the river Gambia, when the whirlwind formed.

Before its appearance there was a dead calm. The preceding days had been very warm, and, since morning, the sky had become covered with heavy clouds. The cutter was in pursuit of a British slaver, when, all at once, those on board of her saw a column of water, about three hundred feet in height, rise from the sea to meet another column (of vapor), descending from the bed of clouds overhead. At this instant, the calm was broken and the storm began to rage furiously. The column in question was not composed of water in its liquid state, but in the condition of very dense vapor, as had been frequently remarked. This column was luminous throughout its whole diameter, and had a slightly yellowish, or tawny, phosphorescent appearance. The sea itself was blazing with light, and the vessel left behind her a long wake of fire. The storm lasted for fourteen hours, and caused many disasters in those waters!"

Navigators frequently have recourse to their guns, in order to break the water-spouts. When the ball passes through them, they are sometimes seen to separate into two parts, which most usually reunite very quickly. Sometimes, on the other hand, the ball simply dashes the water in jets on each side of the column, without affecting it other-

A WATER-SPOUT.

wise in the least. Water-spouts, as Peltier remarks, frequently offer a curious fact, which would seem irreconcilable with the theory of wind tornadoes being the cause of the phenomenon. Many cone-like points start from the clouds and soon combine in one and the same cylinder. It is difficult to demonstrate that different tornadoes thus aggregate in a single shaft, while the attractive forces of electricity may readily enough determine this method of uniting. In the same manner, the cloudy cone is seen dividing into several spirals, which reunite and separate again, a circumstance that sets aside the idea of an impulsion received from the tornadoes of the air.

WHIRLWINDS ON LAND.

Let us now reproduce two accounts of water-spouts on land, that will give an accurate idea of this terrible meteor. The first was observed and described by the learned meteorologist Professor Grossmann:

"On the 25th of June, 1829, about two o'clock in the afternoon, at a point a league below Trèves, east-northeast of Ruwer and Pfalzel, about twenty degrees above the horizon, a phenomenon showed itself that struck a great number of men at work out of doors with amazement, and kept them in uneasy suspense for half an hour.

"A fall of rain had taken place and the sky had remained covered with clouds, when, all at once, from the middle of a black cloud that rose in the east-northeast, a luminous mass began to move in the opposite direction and rend it violently. The cloud speedily assumed, at the top, the form of a chimney, from which escaped a whitish-gray smoke, mingled occasionally with jets of flame, and rising through several openings with as much force as though, to use the expression of the lookers-on, it had been driven by so many bellows.

"The meteor had advanced over the vineyards of Disburg and opposite to Ruwer, when, some distance farther to the south, on the right bank of the Moselle, and completely in contact with the soil, another meteor suddenly appeared. It scattered the heaps of charcoal piled up around a tree, threw down a laborer at an adjacent lime-kiln, and dashed across the Moselle with a terrific concussion, as though a great many stones were shaken together. The water leaped in a column high into the air.

"Continuing to roll along with the same uproar, the meteor, still grazing the ground, darted across the Pfalzel country, leaving everywhere behind it the most evident traces of its zigzag route in the grain-fields and vegetable-patches. Part of the crops was totally destroyed, part was beaten down and torn to pieces, and part whirled away into the air.

"Many women fainted with terror as the meteor passed near them, and others, who were farther off, hid themselves or fled, shrieking that the 'fields were all on fire!' Two laborers, who had climbed a tree, watched the meteor along its entire course; a third had even the bold idea to follow it, which it was easy to do, at the ordinary walking gait. At length, in one of its zigzag movements, it suddenly enveloped him. He felt himself at one moment violently jerked forward, at another tossed up. He then bent down, bracing himself strongly on the ground, with his working-tools; but he was, nevertheless, prostrated. The tornado, however, left him, and passed on its way. The man could recollect no particular impression affecting his smell or taste, but merely a deafening noise. He affirms that there were two currents of air, the one rising obliquely, carrying up with it the stalks and stems of the grain, along with other light bodies, and the second operating in a contrary direction.

" The track that the meteor had opened for itself across the country was, according to different statements, from ten to eighteen paces in breadth and about twenty-five hundred paces in length. Its shape was almost conical, and its color was, at one moment, a grayish-white or yellow, at another a dark-brown, but most of the time a fiery red. The first meteor remained in the air above the second, and followed a nearly parallel route, going toward the north. For about eighteen minutes it presented a large mass of whitish-gray cloud, which repeatedly seemed to vomit flame-colored smoke, and, when seen at the distance of about a mile and a half, had the form of a serpent about one hundred and forty paces long, with its head to the north-northeast and its tail in the opposite quarter.

"In eight or ten minutes, the tail had already changed its position by bending downward. Just at the moment when it was about to touch the head, the whole phenomenon disappeared, and the lower meteor vanished at the same instant, without any detonation from either of them, as an eye-witness affirms; but, with this, a strong smell of sulphur spread over the whole country. Nearly at the same moment, a storm burst forth among the woods situated to the north-northwest of the place where the meteor had appeared, and was accompanied by a fall of extremely large hail-stones.

"The sun was not seen during the whole of this time, as most of the spectators declare, and there was not a breath of wind.

"The upper meteor was seen from Cassel, Gutweiler, and other places, as also at Trèves. It seemed to descend from the heights of Hochwald."

THE TORNADO OF MONVILLE.

The tornado of Monville and Malaunay produced still more fearful effects. The description, incorporated in the *Comptes Rendus* of the French Academy of Sciences, has been summed up by Professor Daguin, of Toulouse, as follows, in his "Treatise of Physics":

"On the 19th of August, 1845, a violent south wind prevailed in the environs of Rouen. In the afternoon, a gust from the southwest, driving some very dark clouds before it, met the southern current, and formed a strong whirlwind, with a sidelong movement that tore up a hundred and eighty bulky trees, twisting and wrenching nearly all of them, and throwing down a drying-house belonging to an adjacent factory. At the same moment, there was a heavy shower accompanied with thunder and hail. However, there was no tornado as yet, properly speaking; but, after receding to a distance and traversing some twenty-five miles, the storm suddenly returned into the valley near Malaunay and Monville, passing through a wood, the trees in which it broke off close to the ground. At that moment, an enormous cone, of sharply-defined outline and as black as coal-smoke, was seen to assume shape. The top of it was of a reddish-yellow, while it emitted flashes of lightning and a heavy rumbling sound. In a few seconds, the tornado hurled itself, with appalling velocity and by zizag motion, through three considerable spinning-mills in succession, crushing them and all the working-people in them. The roofs were swept off, and not one stone left on another. The looms were twisted, the heavy pieces shattered, chiefly, too, where there were ponderous masses of metal. The trees in the vicinity were flung down in every direction, riven and dried up for a length of from six to twenty feet and more. While clearing away the ruins, in the attempt to rescue the unfortunate people buried beneath them, it was noticed that the bricks were burning hot. Planks were found completely charred, and cotton burned and scorched, and many pieces of iron and steel were magnetized. Some of the corpses showed traces of burning, and others had no visible cuts or contusions, but seemed to have been killed by lightning. Workmen who were hurled into the surrounding fields, all agreed in saying that they had seen vivid flashes and had noticed a strong smell of sulphur. Persons who happened to be on the adjacent heights, alleged that they saw the factories wrapped in flames and smoke as the cloud enveloped it. The breadth of the belt laid waste by the tornado was seven hundred and fifteen feet on the level of Malaunay, less than one and a half miles from the point where its ravages began, nine hundred and ninety-five feet in the middle, and one hundred and ninety-five feet near Clères, where the cloud disappeared. The length of the belt, as the bird flies, was about ten miles.

"One really very remarkable circumstance is, that *débris* of all kinds, such as slate, glass, planking, and pieces of wood-work, mingled with cotton, fell near Dieppe, at a distance of from fifteen to twenty-three miles from the scene of the catastrophe. These various objects were beheld in the air by several persons, who mistook them for the leaves of trees, so high were they above the ground. Among the scattered fragments carried thus far, was a scantling more than a yard long, five inches wide, and half an inch thick.

Happily, all such whirlwinds are not so destructive as the one described."

When a thunder-storm changes to a whirlwind, the sound of the thunder ceases at once. The electric discharges are effected through the depressed clouds, and the trees that stand in the track of the meteor. These trees, when traversed by the electricity, are dried up in a moment, and the whirl breaks them instead of tearing them up. The enormous meteor of this kind that laid waste the parish of Chatenay, on the 18th of June, 1839, in this way destroyed the plantations of trees in the valley lying between the hills of Ecouen and the eminence of Chatenay. "Fifteen hundred feet of trees," says Peltier, "had evidently served as conductors to masses of electricity, and to continual, incessant discharges of lightning. The temperature, greatly increased by this flow of the electric fluid, instantaneously vaporized all the moisture in these vegetating conductors, and this vaporization caused every one of them to split lengthwise."

TORNADOES PROPER.

The hurricane-storms, or *cyclones*, during which the wind blows with extraordinary violence, veering at a leap, more or less suddenly, from one point of the horizon to the other, are also classed among those terrific phenomena, the whirling motion of which seems ascribable to an immense electric action. All the descriptions that have been given of them go to show that these meteors are produced like those last described—by beds of thunder-clouds.

The *tornadoes* of the western coast of Africa are sometimes rectilinear gales of wind, like the *pamperos* of South America, and the *arched squalls* of the straits of Malacca, "which rise," says Horsburgh, in his "East India Sailing Directions," "with a black arch of clouds ascending rapidly from the horizon to the zenith, and scarcely giving time to take in sail." But, in most cases, these tornadoes are veritable "cyclones in miniature," as Piddington correctly calls them.

"On the approach of a tornado," says Hopkins, in his work on atmospheric disturbances, "a dense mass of clouds gathers in the east and on the horizon; it is accompanied by frequent, dull, but brief noises, that remind one of the growling of some wild animal. This bank of clouds gradually covers a part of the horizon, and extends from there to the zenith; but generally, beforehand, a small, radiating arch, of well-defined outline, appears on the edge of the horizon, and continually increases. Long before it reaches the ship, one hears the whizzing of the wind, which produces nearly as much noise as the roaring of the thunder when it seems to rend the clouds apart with violence. The course of the gale is distinctly marked by the line of foam that it raises."

The following description, given by Mr. Mingraden in the *Quarterly Journal of Science*, 1837, completes these observations: "When the tornado is approaching, it is remarked that the rain seethes down in torrents, and that the flashes of lightning part the clouds in such profusion that they resemble continual discharges of electric fluid. When, however, the squall has got within half a mile of the ship, these electric appearances cease altogether. The rain only continues the same. When the tornado passes over the vessel, there is a dull crackling distinctly heard in the rigging. It is occasioned by the descent of the electric fluid along the masts, the tips of which serve to attract it; and I have been told that, when this phenomenon occurs at night, every part of the rigging seems illuminated. When the squall has passed the vessel about half a mile, the same signs that characterized its approach from the land reappear exactly, and before attaining the same distance from the ship. The lightnings again descend in continuous sheets, and in such abundance that they resemble the torrents of rain that accompanied the squall. These squalls occur every day during a certain part of the year termed the *harmattan*[1] season. The jet of black clouds, coming from the mountains, begins to appear about nine o'clock in the morning, and reaches the sea about two o'clock in the afternoon. Another singular fact follows these tornadoes. After having whirled over an extent of eight or nine leagues, they disappear, and flashes of lightning are beheld darting up from the sea. The violence of the wind during the storm is excessive.

"The circular motion of the air at the outset of these tornadoes is indicated by the whirling about of the leaves and straws that are caught up by it. These meteors precede the rainy season, and are more or less violent, according to the state of the atmosphere. Ordinarily, they last but a little while, and are always followed by a heavy shower, which revives vegetation, and freshens the atmosphere, that had been made stifling by the blazing heat. Hence, every one feels a vivifying sensation of enjoyment after they are over."

[1] The *harmattan* is a dry wind that blows from the interior of Africa toward the Atlantic, principally in the months of December, January, and February.

CYCLONES.—HURRICANES.

Piddington relates the meeting of two tornadoes, which, in violence, could be compared to cyclones. The phenomenon was observed at Charleston, in South Carolina, May 2, 1761, at two o'clock in the afternoon:

"The tornado crossed the Ashley River, and swooped down upon the shipping at Rebellion Wharf, with such fury as to threaten the destruction of the entire fleet. From the city it was seen coming at first rapidly toward Wappo Creek, like a column of smoke, with a very irregular and tumultuous movement. The quantity of vapor that composed this column, and its prodigious velocity, produced so intense a commotion that it agitated Ashley River to its depths, and left the channel bare. The ebb and flow made the shipping float off to a great distance. When it struck the river, it made a noise like continuous thunder; its diameter, at that moment, was estimated at fifteen hundred feet, and its height, as seen from Charleston, at twenty-five degrees. It was met, at White Point, by another whirlwind, which descended Cooper River, but was not equal to the first. When they came together, the commotion in the air was much greater still; the foam and the vapor seemed to be thrown to the height of forty degrees, while the clouds, that hurried from all directions toward that point, seemed to rush thither and whirl about, at one and the same time, with incredible velocity. The meteor then darted upon the shipping in the roadstead, and reached them in three minutes, although the distance was nearly six miles. Out of forty-five vessels, five were sunk on the spot; the State ship Dolphin and eleven others were dismasted. The damage, estimated at more than £200,000, was done in a moment, and even the vessels that sank were swallowed up so rapidly that the people who were below had scarcely time to scramble up on deck. The whirlwind of Cooper River changed the course of the one that came from Wappo Creek, which, had it not been for that, would, proceeding in the same direction, have swept away the city of Charleston before it like so much straw.

"This terrible column was first perceived about noon, at more than fifty miles west-southwest of the roads. It destroyed every thing in its way, making a complete avenue when it passed through the woods. The loss of the five ships was so sudden that it is not known whether it was the weight of the column of wind, or the mass of water driven upon them, that made them go down."

It is near the Antilles, in the Gulf of Mexico, and in the Indian Seas, that the most disastrous hurricanes burst forth. These are the appalling *cyclones*, during which Nature seems to return to original chaos.

"Sometimes," says an old author, quoted in the article on " Æolian Researches " in the *Nautical Magazine* for 1841, "sometimes, toward that side of the horizon from which the storm comes, is first seen something like a cloud blazing in the most astonishing manner; and some of these hurricanes and whirlwinds have appeared so terrific as to convey the idea that the entire atmosphere and sea were in one tremendous blaze. Captain Prowd, of Stepney, in one of his voyages to the East Indies, encountered a storm of this kind, and left some particulars concerning it, which I have extracted from his journal. The sea was agitated throughout, and what was the most astonishing and terrifying circumstance was, that the sky became surprisingly red and inflamed on the northern part of the horizon. The sun was then at the zenith. Signs of a tempest were recognized in these appearances, and the storm came, as had been foreseen. As the darkness grew thicker, the

A HURRICANE.

violence of the wind increased until it attained the proportions of an awful hurricane. At one o'clock in the morning it beat with such force that it was impossible to keep a sail on the vessel. Seven men could scarcely steer. The whole atmosphere, the sky, and the sea, in their wrath, seemed but one mass of fire."

An official account of the fearful hurricane that devastated Guadeloupe on the 25th of July, 1825, contains the following passage:

" The wind at the moment of its greatest intensity seemed luminous; a silvery flame streamed through the chinks in the walls, the key-holes, and other openings, and made one think, in the darkness inside of the houses, that the heavens were on fire."

Sometimes, a dense bank of clouds of menacing blackness is seen on the side of the horizon from which the cyclone comes. Sheets of lightning issue from it, the "terrible magnificence" of which, according to Piddington, recalls the splendors of the aurora borealis. At the same time, the sea becomes covered with phosphorescent coruscations that fill the sombre night with a pale radiance; while, during the daytime, a blood-red sky spreads its sinister hue over the whole horizon. A profound calm nearly always precedes the hurricane, which is also announced by "the distant moaning of the elements, as though the winds were engulfing themselves in a vault. These remote rumblings recall the sound of a thunder-storm heard in caverns."

The sea assumes a murky color, breaks foaming on the shore, and lifts itself sometimes in enormous tidal-waves ("the heavings of the tempest"), produced by the approach of the cyclone. The elevation of the usual level of the waters, which is almost always the sign of violent storms or heavy rains, often causes inundations of low shores beaten by the hurricane.

The diameter of this immense meteor varies from fifty to one hundred miles, and sometimes more. The disk of whirling air has probably never more than from one to ten miles of vertical height. Placed upon a summit, like the Peak of Teneriffe, the observer would see it pass below him, as travellers among the Alps often view thunder-storms devastating the valleys at their feet. In most of these cases, the disk of the cyclone is so thin that the sky can be distinctly seen through the black masses of cloud. Piddington quotes the following extracts from the log of two sea-captains:

"We observed one very remarkable circumstance: while, all around the horizon, there appeared a bank of dense clouds, the sky at the zenith was so perfectly clear that we could see the stars; and every one on board noticed above the mizzen-mast-head a meteoric light of peculiar brightness.

" While we were lying-to, the clouds were rent asunder, and the sun, gleaming over the whole surface of the water, gave the foam a tinge as white as snow, and then as richly colored as the rainbow in all its shadings."

Numerous observations tend to prove that the disk of the storm is nearly always inclined forward. While the front of the hurricane is attacking the land or the sea, the rear rises, and shows long trains of clouds, which are seen whirling about in the most extraordinary manner. Strong discharges of electricity take place at the same moment and announce the termination of the cyclone.

The typhoons of the India Ocean are preceded by the same signs, and accompanied by the same phenomena, as the cyclones of the Atlantic, from which they differ in some unimportant particulars only. In the China seas, the strongest of these hurricanes are termed "iron whirlwinds."

The frightful sea that they heave up; the

tremendous violence of the wind, blowing in opposite directions from one side to the other of the disk; the dangerous calm that reigns at the centre, and leaves the ship motionless under the shock of monstrous billows; the cataracts of rain; the terrific din of the elements,—all unite to render the struggle hopeless for the seaman. It is especially at night, in the midst of profound darkness, under the livid lightnings, or in the strange phosphorescent glare which sometimes envelops the ship, that the horror of the spectacle defies description. "If the winds are let loose in a tempest," says Thomas Fuller, an old seaman, "they become raging madmen in a hurricane." In his voyage to the Isle of France, Bernardin de Saint-Pierre gives a very exact description of a hurricane that he witnessed:

"On the 23d of December, in the morning, the wind being at the southwest, the weather began to work up for a gale. Clouds accumulated on the summit of the mountains. They were dark, olive, and copper colored. One long upper band that remained motionless was noticed. The clouds lower down were in swift motion. The sea broke with a great noise on the reefs. Many marine birds sought refuge on land and came flying in from the open expanse. The domestic animals seemed uneasy. The air was heavy and warm, although the wind had not fallen. In view of all these signs that foretold a hurricane, everybody hastened to prop and brace his dwelling and carefully to close all the openings.

"About ten o'clock in the evening the tempest came on. First, there were fearful gusts, followed by moments of appalling calm, in which the wind seemed to recruit its strength. Thus it continued with augmenting violence during the night. My cottage having been badly shaken, I moved to another shelter. My hostess was in tears for fear that her house would be destroyed. No one went to bed. Toward morning, the wind having become still more violent, I saw that a whole front of the surrounding palisade was about to fall, and that a portion of our roof was lifting at one corner. So, with some boards and rope, I prevented the damage. In crossing the yard to give some orders, I several times expected to be thrown down. I could see walls falling in the distance, and fragments of ruin carried away, as though they were cards. Rain fell at eight o'clock in the morning, but the wind did not cease. It was driven horizontally with so much violence, that it entered in jets at the smallest orifices.

"At eleven o'clock, the rain fell in torrents. The wind subsided a little, and in ravines of the mountains on all sides prodigious cascades were formed. Pieces of rock detached themselves, and fell with a noise like that of a cannon, and as they rolled down they forced great gaps in the woods. The streamlets overflowed in the plain, which was like a sea.

"At one in the afternoon, the wind leaped round to the northwest, and drove the foam of the sea in huge clouds upon the land. It threw the vessels in port upon the shore, and they kept firing guns of distress, but it was impossible to help them. By those new concussions the houses were shaken in another direction and with nearly equal violence. The winds then made the complete round of the horizon, as is usually the case, and, after that, every thing became quiet again.

"A great many trees were blown down and bridges carried away. Not a leaf was left in the gardens, and even the grass, that strong, coarse, tropical herbage, appeared in some places to have been shaved off close to the ground."

Although these terrible meteors are chiefly frequent in the torrid zone, they also appear sometimes in our temperate climates, on the Atlantic and Mediterranean coasts. We shall presently see how our meteorological observations can follow them in their course, and warn the places menaced by them in good time.

"These convulsions of Nature," says Peltier, "seem necessary to reëstablish the equilibrium of the atmosphere, and often, notwithstanding the terrors that they inspire, the inhabitants of the countries that they ravage invoke them with all their hearts.

"Dense, stagnant fogs, that cause disease, are dispersed by the storm; abundant rains reanimate life and spread freshness on all sides; the air becomes pure and light; renewed by the electric action of these tempests, it restores vigor to men and animals, exhausted by the overwhelming heat of the burning season, and gives back their brilliant verdure to the wilting plants. To the commotion of the hurricane, the howling tempest, the torrents of rain, the lightning, and the thunder, succeed the serenity of the fine weather, the calm, the pure light, and the beauty of an incomparable spring."

CHAPTER VII.

RAINBOWS.—CROWNS AND HALOS.

Description of the Rainbow.—Play of Light in the Drops of Water.—Varied Appearances of the Arch.—Supplementary Arcs.—The Circles of Ulloa.—Crowns.—Colored Arcs.—Parhelia.—White Arcs.—Anthelia.—The Halo of Cléré.

DESCRIPTION OF THE RAINBOW.

"O Thou, Light, eternally one! dwell there, on high, with the Being eternally one! Thou, O changing Color! descend in friendly guise to man!"—SCHILLER.

No scene that Nature presents, better symbolizes this fine thought of the poet than the magnificent arch, painted by the sun upon the dark clouds of a retiring tempest. In all ages, the rainbow has charmed the imaginations and awakened a feeling of hope and consolation in the minds of men. The Hebrew, impressed with the remembrance of the former floods that came upon the earth, felt his soul, that had been disquieted by the thought, resume all its serenity as he beheld

A RAINBOW

the bow of promise. For him it was the token of Jehovah's pardon.

The gay fancy of the Greeks made the rainbow the presage of happy tidings to the earth. the goddess Iris, the messenger of Olympus, according to their creed, left her transparent scarf floating on the clouds.

Ingenious fiction vanished at the approach of science, and the explanation of the rainbow is, to-day, one of the most complete parts we have of the physical theory of light. It is to Kepler, whose genius was prolific in so many directions, that we are indebted for the discovery of the first causes of the phenomenon; he put it on record, although very briefly, in a letter written by him in 1601. Newton studied these causes with all the rigor of geometrical calculation, and was enabled to render an account of all the different modifications observed in the rainbow. After having calculated its dimensions, he verified the correctness of his observations by actual experiment.

We never see the rainbow excepting when standing with our backs toward the sun, the space in front being traversed by a shower of rain, a cascade, or a simple jet of water. When the sea is agitated by a violent wind, and the sun's rays strike the spray of the billows, rainbow curves and arcs are often produced upon it.

Usually, the phenomenon consists of two concentric arches, with a considerable interval between them. The centre of these, as it is easy to prove, corresponds with that point in the heavens where the shadow of the observer's head would fall. The interior curve, which is the oftenest seen, presents a series of prismatic radiations, arranged in such wise that the violet falls inside, and the red upon the outside. In the external curve, the colors of which are much weaker, the order of the series is reversed. Sometimes three bows are seen, but this occurs very rarely. The third, of an extremely pale hue, then presents colors arranged in the same order as in the first instance.

The dimensions of these bows depend upon the height of the sun above the horizon. It must be close to the latter, in order to enable the observer, standing on the surface of the ground, to see arcs, or bows, embracing a half-circumference. It is only from the summits of mountains, or from a balloon high up in the air, that complete circles are visible, unless, as they frequently do, they appear in the spray of great waterfalls. A grand spectacle of this nature is enjoyed in contemplating the magnificent cascade of the Reichenbach. When we

WATERFALL RAINBOWS. p. 173.

saw it, the sun was rising, and the brilliant aërial *coronæ*, or crowns, were floating above the chasm into which the waters plunged. Immense arches of the same kind form upon the white mist that rises over Niagara Falls.

The light of the moon also produces rainbows, but the yellowish reflection that it spreads over all the colors contrasts unfavorably with the vivid hues of the solar bows. The principal arch cannot be seen, and it is difficult to distinguish the variation of the prismatic rays. During a storm which we witnessed on the open sea, we saw a luminous column of the strangest appearance descend from the sky. The ship's crew were struck with terror, and yet the meteor was entirely harmless. The full moon was rising, tinged with red, at that moment, and the column of fire was but a fragment of a rainbow that it reflected on a sheet of rain.

THE PLAY OF LIGHT IN DROPS OF WATER.

All the appearances of the phenomenon of the rainbow show that it is produced by a modification of light taking place in the drops of water. These drops are spherical, and, during a shower, follow each other so rapidly at every point, that we may reason concerning them as though they remained entirely motionless. The ray that penetrates the drop of water is refracted and decomposed. Instead of issuing from it undiminished, as it went in, it reflects itself partly on the concave surface opposite to the point where it entered, and passes back through the globule, until it again meets the surface; there, a similar subdivision takes place. One portion of light passes into the atmosphere, and the other is reflected. By a geometrical diagram, it can be demonstrated that the drops, which may send back to the eye of the observer rays that have been reflected once, or several times, are placed at certain heights, and form circular colored bands, each with a breadth equal to the diameter of the image of the sun. The bands corresponding to a single reflection are at an angular distance of nearly forty degrees from the centre. Those in which the light is reflected twice are nine degrees farther off. In each group, the differences arising from dispersion are small enough to cause the bands to range themselves one above the other, thereby giving rise to the series, sometimes regular and sometimes reversed, of the colors of the spectrum.

There is a simple method of accurately observing the passage of light through drops of water. Suspend a globe of thin glass in a dark room by a cord passing over a pulley. When the globe filled with water is so placed that a ray of light allowed to fall upon it, through an orifice in the window-shutter, forms an angle of nearly forty-two degrees with the line that connects it with the eye, all the colors of the spectrum, commencing with red, can be seen, one after the other, by merely lowering the globe gradually from point to point. If the water be muddy, the passage of the ray can be observed, and we can see that it undergoes but one reflection. When the angle formed by the two lines is fifty-four degrees in measurement, and the ray is made to fall upon the lower part of the globe, the colors are observed to form in like manner, and in the same order, when the globe is gradually elevated. The two reflections can then be easily distinguished in the water.

According to the explanation thus given, the rainbow is found to be purely a local phenomenon. Each spectator sees a different arch. If the rainy cloud be near, two observers, placed at some distance from each other, see the ends of their rainbows resting on different points of the ground. This fact is particularly evident when one is standing opposite to a mountain upon which the bow is projected.

VARIOUS ASPECTS OF THE BOW.—SUPPLEMENTARY ARCS.

The rays of the sun may happen to be reflected toward a cloud from the surface of a placid expanse of water, and this reflection also may produce a rainbow. Calculation shows that, in such a case, this arch must cut the arch directly formed, at a height that depends upon the elevation of the luminary. When these two phenomena produce a secondary arch, the four curves, thus interlaced, offer a very beautiful sight. Monge narrates an instance where they were complete in form and perfectly distinct. Halley once saw three arcs, one of which was formed by rays reflected from the surface of a river. The latter arc first intersected the external arc in such manner as to divide it into three equal parts. When the sun descended toward the horizon, the points of contact drew closer together. Ere long there was but one, and, as the colors were in reversed order in the two rainbows, a space of perfect white was formed at this sole point by the superposition of the two series. The sun, when high enough above the horizon, may, when reflected from a sheet of water, form a complete circle. Sometimes the upper part is wanting, and then there remains the singular phenomenon of a rainbow reversed.

Supplementary arcs are often seen when the rainbow is very brilliant. We give this name to colored bands observed inside of the interior and outside of the exterior arch. After the violet, is usually seen red, then green, and then violet again. These colors may even be repeated several times in the same order. It is on the culminating part of the arch, and only when the latter is very high, that this phenomenon occurs. It is explained by the laws of optics that relate to refraction; in other words, the modifications that light undergoes in grazing the surface of bodies.

THE CIRCLE OF ULLOA.

Rainbows, in which the colors were extremely faint, have been observed in dense fogs. This appearance arises from the diminutive size of the drops of moisture. The great whitish ring, or circle, seen by Ulloa and Bouguer during their stay on the Pichincha, seems to have had this origin. It has been called the White Rainbow, or the Circle of Ulloa. Its dimensions are those of the main arch usually seen, and it is perceived only from elevated places, simultaneously with the formation of rainbow-like halos around shadows projected on the fog. We have reproduced the description of this phenomenon given by Bouguer, and will add what Ulloa says of it:

"He was on Pambamarca with six companions at daybreak. The top of the mountain was entirely covered with dense clouds. As the sun rose, it dispelled these clouds, and nothing remained in their stead but some very light mists, which it was almost impossible to distinguish. Suddenly, on the side opposite that in which the sun rose, each of the travellers saw, at a dozen fathoms from where he stood, an image of himself reflected in the air, as though upon a mirror. This image appeared in the centre of three rainbows shaded with different colors, and surrounded at a certain distance by a fourth arch of a single color. The tinting farthest on the outside of each arch was flesh-colored, or red, the next shade was orange, the third was yellow, the fourth straw-color, and the last one green. All these arcs were perpendicular to the horizon; they moved about and followed the person reflected in every direction, surrounding his image like a gloria. What was most remarkable was, that, although the seven travellers stood together in a single group, each of them saw the phenomenon only in relation to himself, and was disposed to deny its

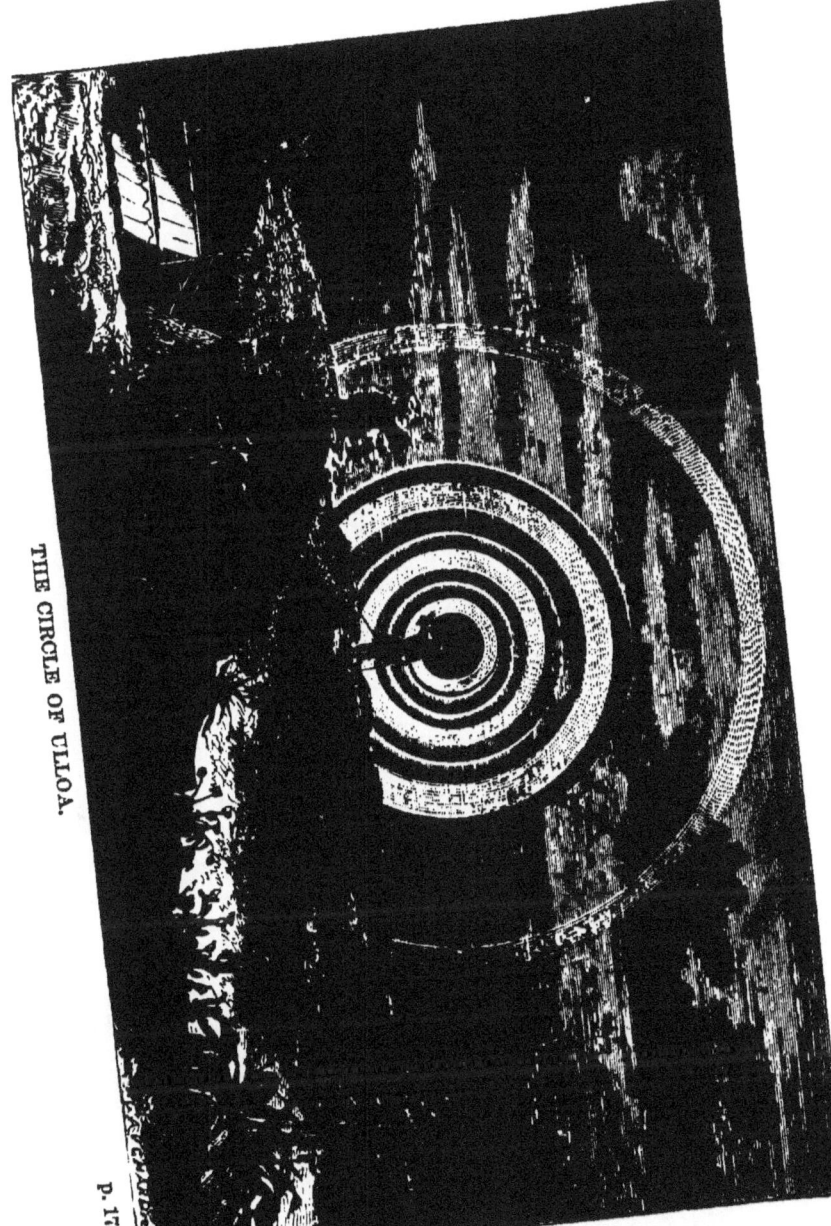

THE CIRCLE OF ULLOA.

existence in reference to the others. The extent of these arches increased progressively in proportion to the height of the sun. At the same time their colors faded away, the *spectra* became paler and paler and more vague, and at last the phenomenon entirely disappeared. When this display began, the shape of the arcs was oval; and, toward the last, it was perfectly circular.

CROWNS, OR CORONÆ.

When light clouds pass over the sun or the moon, there may be perceived around those luminaries one or more colored circles, known to meteorology as crowns. In all these circles, we distinguish the prismatic colors, the violet being placed inside and the red outside. They are at an equal distance from each other, but this distance varies according to the condition of the clouds and the atmosphere. The angular diameter of the first circle is ordinarily comprised in from one to four degrees.

"All clouds," says Kaemtz, "that are not too thick to let the light of the sun pass through them, the *cirrus* and the *cirro-stratus* excepted, present traces of crowns, but the brightness of the colors is not always the same. I have never seen them so handsome as upon fogs which form, during the night, in the valleys, and ascend, toward the middle of the day, to the summits of the mountains. When strips of cloud passed between the sun and me, the colors had a vividness which I have rarely seen in them. They are no less fine on the cirro-cumulus, particularly when they are in small masses of dazzling whiteness, and so confused on their edges that it is difficult to trace their outlines on the sky."

This phenomenon is, in its turn, explained by the refraction of luminous rays passing near the globules of water that compose the clouds. A very simple experiment gives us an imitation of the process. We have only to hold up before a lamp a strip of glass besprinkled with lycopodium, or vegetable sulphur. The fine grains of the latter substance, acting as globules do, the flame of the lamp is at once surrounded by prismatic rings, separated by equal intervals.

COLORED HALOS.—PARHELIA.

In the phenomena of which we are about to treat, small crystallizations of ice, and not globules of water, modify the light. We are sometimes surrounded by fogs formed of such particles. They frequently exist, as aëronauts have ascertained, in the higher regions of the atmosphere, where they form the clouds called *cirrus*.

If the play of the luminous rays in the little spheres we have been considering has given us such pleasing phenomena, we may readily comprehend that, when they pass through limpid crystals with numerous facets, we shall have fresh, harmonious combinations of geometrical lines and of colors to admire.

In temperate climates, the phenomena of this order most frequently remarked are the halos, or colored circles, that surround the sun or the moon, but in a manner different from crowns. The arrangement of the colors of the spectrum is usually reversed in them, the red being placed inside. The distances of the circles from the luminary are equable, and much greater than in the corona. Thus, the interior halo is from twenty-two to twenty-three degrees in diameter; the second halo, usually called the external one, measures forty-six, and the third ninety-nine degrees in diameter. Brewster imitated the halo by placing a strip of glass, covered with crystallized alum, before a lamp. In order thoroughly to comprehend the formation of this phenomenon, we must suppose a very great number of prismatic needles suspended in the air. These prisms, in certain positions, may revolve for a considerable period on their own centres, without the deviation of the refracted rays changing perceptibly. The multiplicity of these rays proceeding in any one direction, giving the eye a more vivid expression, colored belts, or bands, are seen placed one above the other, as in the rainbow.

When the sun or the moon is near the horizon, and the atmosphere remains calm, the needles of ice arrange themselves vertically, and brilliant spots, diffused images of the luminary, are formed along the horizontal diameter of the halo and a little outside of each circle. These take the name of *parhelia*, or *paraselenæ*. Parhelia, those of the interior halo especially, are finely colored, all the shadings of the spectrum following the red, which is next to the sun. When the latter luminary rises, the spots withdraw from the circles, remaining, however, on the line of the horizontal diameter.

Sometimes we see, resting upon the halos, what are termed tangential arcs, or arches of contact, of very brilliant color. The most frequent are those that form symmetrically at the extremities of the vertical diameter of the halo, of twenty-three degrees. Those of the external halo, which are more rare, but more numerous at the time,

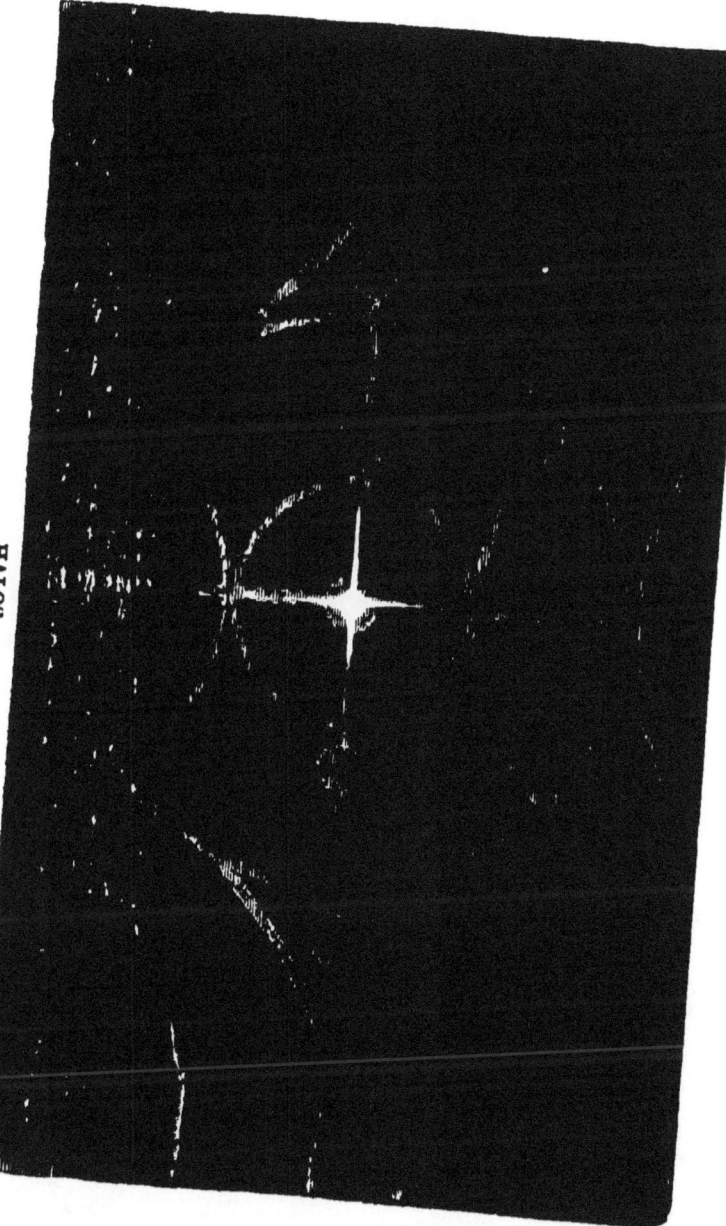

HALOS.

p. 182.

touch it, not only in the vertical line of the sun, but also at the lateral points forty-five degrees distant. The most elevated of these arches, which has the zenith of the observer for its pole, is sometimes designated by the name of the *circum-zenithal circle.*

We cannot, here, enter into details as to the manner in which these appearances are produced by the refraction of light in the crystals. M. Bravais, in his learned researches on this subject, did not confine himself to calculating all the circumstances of the phenomenon; he succeeded in reproducing it artifically, in a dark room, by means of an ice-prism, which he caused to revolve very rapidly while the rays of the sun were projected upon it.

WHITE ARCS.—ANTHELIA.

The appearances that we have now to describe are always entirely white, a fact indicating that they result, not from the passage of light through the crystals, but from its reflection from their facets. Their brightness is variable, sometimes exhibiting only pallid gleams of light, and sometimes a dazzling splendor like that of the central luminary. First, an immense circle, called the *parheliac circle*, crosses the sun or the sky, making the two halos intersect each other, and spanning the whole horizon at an invariable height. Upon this circle, and opposite to the sun, its image is reproduced alone, or accompanied by two others, which take their places symmetrically beside it. Sometimes these images, or *anthelia*, are crossed by two white arches, which extend to a considerable distance. *Vertical columns* are also seen to form, in other words, luminous trains, that extend twenty-five degrees above and below the luminary, thus forming, with a portion of the parheliac circle, a cross, with limbs more or less unequal.

According to the *savant* Babinet, an imitation of the parheliac circle is produced when the sun is looked at through a crystal of fibrous structure, cut in laminæ parallel to its fibre, and placed in a vertical position. The white horizontal belt which is then seen results from the coruscation of these fibres. Bravais has explained this phenomenon, as well as those of the *anthelia* and their arcs, by means of his ingenious apparatus.

Some physiologists attribute to the effects of the mirage, the *false suns* and false moons that are sometimes seen beside the real luminary when it is near the horizon, but the same phenomena may be explained by the interposition of an infinite number of small crystals composed of prisms and pyramids.

We shall not enter further into details of the appearances that halos present. We should have to add other curves and other disks, due to quite infrequent crystalline combinations, and we should become involved in too many complex forms and colors. Let us merely add, that very brilliant parhelia and arches themselves become sometimes sources of light that cause similar duplicate phenomena, which, however, are naturally very faint.

In the illustration given are seen the principal parts of halos. We must suppose the white horizontal belt to be prolonged to the side of the heavens opposite the sun, where the image of that luminary is repeated several times. But the phenomenon scarcely ever has its complete development. Sometimes it is one and sometimes another form of crystals that is produced in the atmosphere, and these diminutive bodies float there, or descend slowly, in different positions, accordingly as the air is calm or agitated. The parts that we have represented are, consequently, seen together but seldom, and it is not surprising, therefore, to find a great variety of different accounts by different observers.

It is generally noticed that the sky, on the inside of the halo of twenty-three degrees, is in striking contrast, by its dark-gray color, with the general illumination of the external space. This peculiarity is explained by the direction of certain rays, refracted by the prisms which produce the halo. As in rainbows, there is a great difference in brightness between the solar and the lunar halos. In the latter, the colors are always very dull, but the white parts of the great geometrical figure, when it is formed, always throw back a beautiful silvery light.

THE HALO OF CLÉRÉ.

A remarkable display of halos and *paraselenæ* was observed on February 21, 1864, at eight o'clock in the evening, in many localities of the Departments of Indre-et-Loire and Loire-et-Cher, in France.

"It was at Cléré that the phenomenon presented the most curious appearance.

"The sky was clear and cloudless, and even the stars could be seen, notwithstanding the moonlight.

"All at once, rays of a silvery white, darting apparently from the moon, described a Greek cross, of which the moon occupied the centre. A white ring of a deeper tinge connected the arms of the cross, and thus formed a first and magnificent lunar halo.

"At each arm, one extending to the north and the other to the south, and at equal distances from them, the image of the moon was reproduced by a luminous globe of the same size, half white, and half tinged with the colors of the rainbow. These globes sometimes darted out luminous rainbow-colored rays, like the tail of a comet.

"A second halo, in an immense circle outside of the first one, and starting from the luminous globes that tipped the arms of the cross, surrounded the borough of Cléré. It was of exactly the same color as the first one. This second halo also displayed two luminous globes, in all respects similar to the first pair, at an equal distance on its circumference. Thus, there were five luminous globes, including the moon, all connected by the rings and the branches of the cross.

"What was still more curious was, that two crescents of unequal size, and placed at a certain distance one above the other, occupied the centre of the second halo above the cross, without any direct association with the rest of the phenomenon."

At Mettray, the appearance was as follows: "The silvery circle around the moon was cut by two perpendicular luminous diameters. One of these, running northeast and southwest, exhibited at each extremity the hues of the rainbow. These two points, thus rich in coloring, projected of themselves, beyond the circle, a long, luminous, but colorless train, affecting the form of part of an ellipse.

"The phenomenon passed through different phases, in consequence of the displacement of the clouds, or more probably of the snowy mass interposed between the moon and the eye of the spectator.

"The luminous diameters disappeared slowly, and the circle became gradually depressed, so as to assume a completely elliptical form. The curve at the same time became tinted with the colors of the rainbow, but dimmer than they, while the two extremities of the long diameter, which had been prismatically variegated since the first appearance of the halo, continued to show great luminous intensity."

To conclude: at Amboise, the phenomenon presented features no less remarkable:

"In fine, clear weather, that left the stars plainly distinguishable, the full moon however being slightly clouded, there gradually appeared a halo, or luminous circle, of considerable dimensions, with the moon in the centre. At the same time, another circle formed, no less in breadth than the first one, but much greater in upward length, and the moon occupied a point in its circumference, to the southward. The two circles intersected each other, and the refracted light being in some sort accumulated at the two points of intersection, situated to the eastward and westward of the moon, two luminous foci were seen there, which gradually displayed all the colors of the rainbow, perfectly visible and perfectly distinct."

CHAPTER VIII.

THE AURORAL LIGHTS.

General Description.—Icy Fog.—Noise and Odor.—Electrical Currents.—Magnetic Influence.—The Aurora Australis.—Different Points of View.—Periodicity of the Auroral Lights.

GENERAL DESCRIPTION.

MANY hours, and sometimes a whole day, before the appearance of the *aurora borealis*, irregular movements are observed in the magnetic needle. During that time its deviation to the west, or declination, sensibly augments. Little by little, toward the north, the atmosphere thickens along the horizon, and a curtain of violet mists, thin enough to let the stars be seen through them, begins to ascend. Its upper border brightens feebly at first, and then this illumination becomes more and more regular, and forms an arch of a pale-yellow hue, turning its concavity toward the earth, and with its summit in the meridian.

This arch ascends slowly, and gradually be-

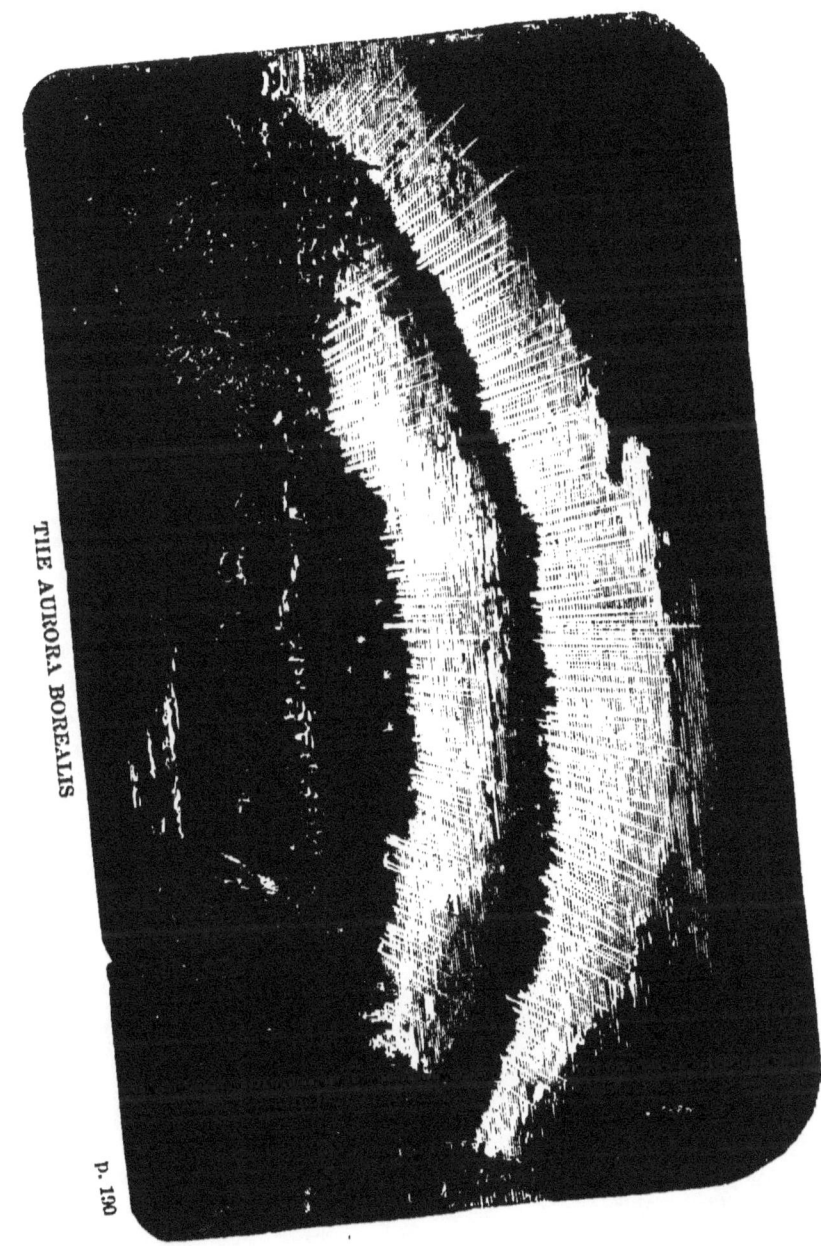

THE AURORA BOREALIS

p. 130

comes more luminous. Striated rays of blackish tint assume shape, and a sort of effervescence is observed along the entire extent of the arch. Ere long, other rays shoot up of various length and brightness, and dart into the sky, like rockets. The fiery train, which at times is dazzling, passes from purply-red to emerald-green, but most usually a magnificent yellow tinge predominates.

In their upward flight, these rays go beyond the zenith, and seem to converge toward the same point in the sky, namely, the magnetic zenith, indicated by the prolongation of a magnetic needle freely suspended.

In order to depict the suddenness of the variations of light in the rays, Bravais, like ourselves, says that they *dart*. Occasionally, they are so multiplied that they invade the entire celestial vault, forming an immense cupola of fire, agitated like the billows of the sea. No description could do justice to the splendor of this spectacle.

With the first streaks of the aurora, the magnetic needle is subjected to lively oscillations. These augment when the rays appear. Each one of them, as it shoots from the arch, makes the compass, in some sort, palpitate, and then sailors say that it is *bewitched*. Intervals of tranquillity, that grow more and more frequent, next mark the declining phase of the aurora, and it has been ascertained that the deviation of the needle then takes place in the inverse ratio of its declination when the phenomenon began.

M. Lottin, intrusted, in common with M. Bravais, with a scientific mission to Iceland, describes a remarkable undulating motion that may be noticed in the auroral beams when watched attentively.

" While the arch," says he " is ascending toward the zenith, with every additional foot, the brightness of each beam successively gathers intensity. This kind of luminous current displays itself several times in succession, and much more frequently from west to east than in the opposite quarter. Sometimes, but rarely, a retrograde movement takes place immediately after the first one, and as soon as the glow has run through all the beams, one after the other, from west to east, it changes to the opposite direction, thereby returning to its point of departure, without our being able to say whether it is the rays that are thus carried across by a nearly horizontal movement, or this brighter light speeding from one beam to the other, step by step, without the latter undergoing any displacement."

We shall see, further on, that this appearance

arises, in reality, from a transfer of the beams themselves.

Sometimes, when the ends of the auroral arch have left the horizon, and it is rising higher in the sky, the alternate motion of the rays attached to it make it look like a long, golden drapery floating in the atmosphere, folding and reopening in a thousand ways, and undulating as though agitated by the wind. This first arch fades and dies out by degrees as it ascends, but, in the mean time, new ones present themselves, some of them commencing diffusely, and others with beams already formed. Nine arches have been counted at one time, forming in this manner, and passing through nearly the same phases.

In the region toward which the beams converge, there often appears a luminous, elliptical curve, called the boreal *corona*, or crown. It seems to be merely an effect of perspective. The rays, running parallel to the magnetic needle freely suspended, are disposed like the ridges of a cylindrical tunnel, which are seen converging toward the centre of the two openings. When this corona appears, the aurora is in its complete development. It does not remain long visible, however, and the phenomenon soon enters upon its declining phase. The beams become more sparse, shorter, and less vividly colored. "Bundles of rays," says M. Lottin, "belts, and fragments of arcs, appear and disappear at intervals. Then the beams become more and more diffused, until they are seen only as vague and feeble gleams, which, at last, spread over the whole firmament, grouped together like small *cumuli*, and designated by the name of *auroral flakes*. Their milky-white radiance often undergoes very vivid changes of intensity, similar to dilating and contracting movements, which are propagated from the centre to the circumference, and recall those of the marine animals known as *medusæ*. The twilight phase comes on, little by little, and the phenomenon, gradually fading away, at length ceases to be visible. At other times, the rays still appear at daybreak, and then suddenly vanish; or, as the morning twilight grows brighter, they become more vague, assume a whitish color, and end by commingling and losing themselves in the cirro-stratus, in such manner that it is impossible to distinguish them from that species of cloud."

ICE-FOGS.

Our remarks, just made in reference to the last phase of auroras, indicate their relations with the clouds composed of small crystals of ice. It is very easy to make out, by daylight, those foggy points in the sky which were seen in the form of auroral flakes, while they were illuminated by electricity, which is the first cause of the phenomenon. Sometimes, also, trains of *cirrus* are perceived in the region where the most brilliant beams were seen. Admiral Wrangel remarked that halo arches formed around the moon at the moment when auroral rays darted in the direction of that luminary.

"During the daytime," said Humboldt, "clouds sometimes group together, and arrange themselves almost like the rays of an *aurora borealis*, and then they seem to disturb the magnetic needle." Father Secchi, the director of the observatory at Rome, has also established the fact that magnetic perturbations manifest themselves at night when light phosphorescent clouds veil the heavens. These are, in a certain degree, feeble *auroræ*. Every body has had a chance to notice the *Polar belts* described by Humboldt. These clouds are disposed in long parallel lines in the direction of the magnetic meridian, and are seen quite frequently in our climates. M. de Tessan, in his account of the voyage of the Venus, reports that one of the officers of the frigate always predicted fine auroras from having observed the arrangement of the cirrus during certain days.

In Canada, meteorological registers have been kept, for a long time, which indicate the state of the atmosphere on days that precede and follow auroral displays. On nearly all those days there has been either snow or rain, a circumstance which renders it very probable that icy particles were in the atmosphere during the presence of the aurora. This infinite quantity of extremely delicate crystals, traversed by electric currents, constitutes, as it were, an immense luminous net-work floating in the atmosphere.

It must be borne in mind that all these delicate needles of ice may exist in the air while the sky continues to look perfectly serene. Doctor Richardson, in fine weather, and at a temperature of thirty-two degrees (centigrade) below zero, saw the arc of the aurora in the neighborhood of the zenith, and, at the same moment, remarked the fall of an extremely fine snow, which was scarcely visible, but which left drops on his hand in melting.

The existence of the fog that is seen on the horizon, in the form of a darkish segment, before the commencement of this luminous phenomenon, confirms the preceding observations. In northern countries, travellers have found themselves, when on the summits of mountains, suddenly enveloped in a transparent mist of a grayish color, bordering on green, which then became transformed, in a higher region, to a splendid aurora borealis.

NOISE AND ODOR.—ELECTRIC CURRENTS.

When the point of observation is sufficiently near the aurora, there is heard a peculiar rustling sound, mixed with sudden crackling noises, analogous to those produced by electricity when it escapes from a body in the form of an *aigrette* or a sheaf. Frequently a sulphurous smell is in the air, and this is due, no doubt, to the ozone which is produced during the electric discharges of the pole, as it is in a thunder-storm.

When treating of storms, we said that the atmosphere is constantly charged with positive electricity, produced in great part in the tropical regions. The earth, on the contrary, is negatively electrified, and a neutralization is effected by means of the humidity of the lower strata of the atmosphere. Says De la Rive, to whom we are indebted for this theory: "It is principally in the polar regions, where the eternal ices condense the aqueous vapors incessantly in the form of fog, that this neutralization should take place; and, with the greater reason, that the positive vapors are borne thither and accumulated by the tropical current, which, starting from the equatorial regions, where it occupies the highest range of the atmosphere, descends as it advances toward the more elevated latitudes, until, in the vicinity of the poles, it comes in contact with the earth. It is there, then, that the discharge of the positive electricity of the mists, and the negative electricity of the earth, should essentially take place, with an accompaniment of light, when it is intense enough, if, as is almost always the case near the poles, and sometimes in the upper parts of the atmosphere, it encounters in its course particles of ice of extreme tenuity which form the fogs and clouds very high up in the air."

According to the more or less foggy condition of the atmosphere in the polar regions, and therefore its greater or inferior capacity as a conductor, the two electricities more or less readily neutralize each other. Hence arise currents of variable intensity that traverse the surface of the earth from the pole to the equator. It is the influence of these currents upon the magnetic needle which produces the deviations and oscillations that we have signalized.

These perturbations are continual in the highest latitudes, because the intensity of the electric currents is greater, and their influence more marked. In proportion as we descend toward the equator, we notice fewer deviations, but still they take place to some extent everywhere, even in places where the aurora is not visible. For several years Arago, in following the variations of the needle at the observatory of Paris, was able to announce the appearance of the aurora borealis in the Eastern Hemisphere, without being once mistaken.

During the fine aurora of November 27, 1848, Signor Mateucci observed the influence of the currents in a very remarkable form. He writes: "I was at the electric-telegraph office in Pisa, when we were suddenly surprised by the apparatus ceasing to work, although it had always operated perfectly well in the daytime. The same thing happened at the same moment in Florence. We tried to make it go by increasing the force of the currents, and then by acting upon the manipulators; but all in vain,—the anchor remained attached to the electro-magnets." This singular effect ceased when the aurora disappeared, and the apparatus again performed its task as perfectly as ever. In England, Mr. Highton has recorded the very prolonged effect of the aurora upon the telegraph-wires.

In all parts of the European net-work of telegraphs the working of the wires was disturbed by the magnificent aurora of August 28, 1859. Two days later, the luminous phenomenon was perceived over a great part of the continents of Europe, Asia, and America, and a magnetic action still more general was noticed. There were currents sufficiently intense to cause a spark to be thrown off when they were interrupted. In the United States, two telegraph-operators, stationed at Boston and Portland, were able to use the terrestrial fluid, which was much more powerful than that of the machine, and kept up a conversation for some time.

MAGNETIC INFLUENCE.

Let us now consider the great mass of luminous fog placed in the icy zone, and acting as a species of movable conductor traversed by a succession of electrical discharges. The globe being considered a huge magnet, what is the action of the magnetic pole upon this fog?

To M. de la Rive we are indebted for a very interesting experiment in physics, which has put us in a way to solve this problem. He took a hollow ball of glass, in which the air was extremely rarefied, and arranged inside of it an apparatus causing jets of electric light to converge upon the pole of an electro-magnet. He states the result as follows: "As soon as the cylinder of soft iron, which serves for an electro-magnet, is magnetized, the electric light, instead of starting indifferently from different points of the upper surface, which serves as a pole, as it did before being magnetized, parts from all the points of the circumference of that surface, in such manner as to form a sort of continuous luminous ring around it. That ring has a kind of rotary movement around the magnetized cylinder, sometimes in one direction and sometimes in another, according to the direction of the discharge, and the sense in which the magnetizing was done. Finally, some jets of light more brilliant than the rest seem to shoot forth from this luminous circumference, without becoming confounded with the rest of the sheaf of rays. As soon as the magnetic state ceases, the luminous phenomenon becomes what it was before."

Relying upon this experiment, M. de la Rive constructed an apparatus consisting of a wooden sphere, with a covering of soft iron, to represent the earth. With this apparatus he was able to reproduce not only the polar auroræ but also the different effects that they determine, such as the disturbance of the magnetic needle and the movements of electricity in the telegraphic wires.

We have said that the arc of the *aurora borealis* always has its summit placed in the magnetic meridian. In the great aurora of the autumn of 1859, the arc appeared to have its centre toward the northwest in California, nearly at the north in Philadelphia, and toward the northwest in England. This would place the real centre in North America. A great number of like observations have led to the same result, and the auroræ thus present themselves to us as luminous rings of variable diameter, centred around the magnetic pole, and hovering at a greater or less height in the atmosphere, shooting forth vertical rays. The undulating movement of the arch, and of the radiations emanating from it, described by M. Lottin, which would seem to indicate their rotation from the west to the east, passing up by the south, adds another feature of resemblance between the great phenomenon and the experiment of M. de la Rive. In fact, it is in this sense that the ring should turn when the positive electricity issuing from the atmosphere is directed toward the north magnetic pole.

The form and movements of the aurora are

therefore determined by the forces which emanate from the grand terrestrial magnet. And we may add a remarkable observation of M. Hansteen: "During the aurora, and for several days afterward, the magnetic intensity is notably diminished, and recovers its usual value only by degrees."

THE AURORA AUSTRALIS.

Judging from such few observations as have been collected in the southern hemisphere, it may be said that the aurora australis, or southern aurora, presents the same phenomena as the aurora borealis. It is explained in a similar manner. Several cases of coincidence between the illuminations of the two poles have been remarked.

M. de Tessan has given the following description of a southern aurora, observed during the voyage of the Venus: "On January 20, 1839, at twenty minutes past one o'clock in the morning, we noticed a fine aurora forming a very apparent and clearly-marked luminous arc of a circle. Its radiance was white; there may, however, have been a slight greenish tinge, for it reminded one somewhat of the light of a phosphorescent body. This light was soft and steady, and might be compared, as to brightness, with that of the upper edge of a cloud of the cumulus order from behind which the moon is just emerging. Flashes, or beams, equally white, but of much less intensity, rose from different points of the arc. These flashes appeared and disappeared, very perceptibly, in the same place, after a variable duration of from five to ten minutes.

"The lower part of the arc seemed to be occupied by a large black cloud, the borders of which, adjacent to the arc, were slightly notched. I took this appearance for a real cloud; I noted it as such, and not a doubt on the subject would have entered my mind, had I not, since my return, seen similar appearances cited as deceptive by skilful observers, who assure us that they could see the stars through this apparently dense cloud.

"The sky was quite clear, and only dotted with a few large clouds, while the stars were very brilliant. We heard no particular noise from the direction of the aurora."

DIFFERENT POINTS OF VIEW.—THE PERIODICITY OF AURORAS.

Frequently, observers at the north have found themselves placed in the middle of the aurora, below the luminous ring. At that time the arch extended beyond the zenith, and in a great measure concealed the trajectory of the rays. It is in these conditions that the noise of the electric discharges becomes perceptible, as well as the smell of ozone. The curious circumstance has been remarked, that the magnetic needle remains completely motionless there, while it is keenly agitated everywhere else on the surface of the globe. The direction assigned by theory to the currents accounts for this effect.

In our middle latitudes, the aurora borealis usually displays itself in a coloring of the sky, which looks like the reflection of a conflagration. We likewise, but less often, see large, reddish clouds, from which sometimes shoot forth beams that ascend to the zenith. Before this meteor was completely understood, and admired for its beauty, and for the solace afforded by its brilliant illumination during the long polar nights, it was in Europe a source of terror. In antiquity and the middle ages, those red flames, those shooting rays, seemed blazing torches, and swords dipped in blood. The imagination at one time depicted an immense conflict, in which men of fire struggled for mastery; and, at another, an assemblage of hideous heads tossing their flaming tresses.

The aurora borealis is not always visible. It is, very probably, a phenomenon that frequently occurs in the daytime. During a winter passed at Bossecop, in the seventieth degree of latitude, M. Lottin counted one hundred and fifty auroræ in two hundred nights. Naturally, the number of appearances of the phenomenon grows smaller as we recede more and more from the magnetic pole.

An annual periodicity has been remarked in the visible auroræ, the number of which increases as we approach the equinoxes, and diminishes at the epoch of the solstices. These fluctuations must depend upon the greater or less abundance of vapors carried toward the poles during different seasons. At the equinoxes, circumstances are perceptibly the same in the two hemispheres, and it is also at this epoch that the simultaneousness of the boreal and austral auroræ has been noted.

CHAPTER IX.

SHOOTING-STARS.

Fire-balls.—Showers of Stones.—Meteoric Stones.—An Extraordinary Meteor.—Velocity and Appearance of Fire-balls.—The Fall of Aërolites.—Periodical Reappearances.—Composition of Aërolites.—Darkening of the Sun.—Ring of Meteorites.

FIRE-BALLS.

EVERY one has seen the luminous furrows of various colors, direction, and extent, which are rapidly traced across the constellations, sometimes by brilliant luminous points without apparent diameter, and sometimes by globes of fire of divers dimensions. The latter, which are spoken of as fire-balls, or *bolides*, sometimes split into pieces at the end of their course, with a loud report, and leaving a small cloud at the point where they disappeared.

Dazzling trains of light and blazing *bolides* have been seen in broad daylight, but very rarely. During the night an average of ten shooting-stars per hour is seen, but, in certain seasons of the year, they cross the heavens in swarms, and numerous fire-balls are sometimes interspersed with these great displays.

Divers causes have been assigned for these phenomena. Kepler believed them to be engendered by "terrestrial exhalations," and this opinion has been handed down to our day, with but little modification. Most *savants*, however, have adopted another way of accounting for them. They attribute all these meteors to mineral masses known by the name of aërolites, which, when they fall to the ground, exhibit traces of intense combustion. A passage in Plutarch shows that the ancients had adopted that explanation:— "Some philosophers," he says, in his life of Lysander, "think that shooting-stars do not arise from detached parts of ether coming to extinguish themselves in the air, immediately after taking fire; nor do they spring from the atmosphere in a state of dissolution, in great quantity, in the upper regions; they are rather heavenly bodies that fall to the earth, or, in other words, bodies withdrawn in some manner from the force of rotation, and precipitated, not only upon the inhabited regions, but upon the great seas, whence it comes that they are not afterward found."

Diogenes of Apollonius mentions a star of stone that fell "all on fire near Ægos Potamos." The fall of this aërolite made a great impression on the inhabitants of Thrace. According to the description that has remained to us, it was twice the size of an ordinary millstone, and made a whole wagon-load by itself. A shower of stones fell near Rome during the reign of Tullus Hostilius. In Galatia, Cybele was worshipped in the form of a stone that had fallen from the sky. At Emesis, in Syria, a similar stone was set apart for the worship of the sun. These two meteoric stones were subsequently transported to Rome.

SHOWERS OF STONES.

Even as late as the eighteenth century, learned men did not believe in stones falling from the sky. It was only in 1794 that Chladni attempted to demonstrate the truth of the explanation which had been stowed away among popular superstitions. Not long afterward, in 1803, on the 26th of April, a shower of stones fell upon the small town of Laigle, in Normandy, and dispelled all doubt on the subject. A regular statement was drawn up, and the messenger of the Institute who went to the spot made a report, which Humboldt has quoted in his "Cosmos," as follows:

"At one o'clock in the afternoon, with the sky perfectly clear, a large fire-ball was seen from Alençon, Falaise, and Caen, moving through the air from southeast to northwest. Shortly afterward there was heard at Laigle, for four or five minutes, an explosion coming from a small and almost motionless black cloud. This was followed by three or four others, and a noise that one would imagine was produced by discharges of musketry mingled with the rolling of a great number of drums. Each explosion detached from the black cloud some of the vapors that formed it. At that point no luminous phenomenon was observed. More than two thousand meteoric stones, of which the largest weighed seventeen pounds, fell upon an elliptical surface ranging from southeast to northwest, and about eleven kilometres in length. These stones smoked, they were burning hot, without being on fire, and it was ascertained that it was easier to break them within a few days after their fall than at a later period."

METEORIC STONES.

Popular tradition being thus confirmed by actual experience, all that could be remembered of the observations of the ancients was brought together, and efforts were made to collect new ones. Howard, an English chemist, drew up a chronological list of all the stones that had thus fallen from the sky since the earliest times. This list Chladni has completed. We select from it the most remarkable instances that can be referred to a determinate epoch:

Before the Christian Era.—The thunder-stone that fell in Crete, and was held in veneration as the symbol of Cybele.—The sudden shower of stones which destroyed the enemies of the Jewish people at Beth-horon, as told by Joshua.—The sacred shield that fell in the reign of Numa.—The black stone kept in the Kaaba, at Mecca.—The thunder-bolt, hard and glittering, from which the sword of Antar was fashioned.

After the Christian Era.—Fall of a stone weighing two hundred and sixty pounds at Ensisheim, in Alsace. This enormous stone was kept for a long time on the altar of the village church.—A stone of black metallic color, of the size and form of a human head, and weighing fifty-four pounds, fell on Mount Vaison, in Provence.—A stone fell in a fishing-boat in Copensha.—A stone fell at Larissa, in Macedonia; this stone, which emitted a sulphurous odor, and had the appearance of iron in ebullition, weighed sixty-two pounds.—

A great shower of stones at Barbotan, near Roquefort. Some of the fragments were from twenty-eight to thirty pounds in weight; one of them penetrated a cabin and killed a shepherd and a young bull.—A shower of stones at Cutro, in Calabria, during the fall of a great quantity of red dust.—Stony masses fell in the Baltic Sea just after the great Gottenburg meteor.

At four o'clock, in the afternoon of the 13th of September, 1768, there was seen at the village of Luce, two leagues from Chartres, in France, a dark cloud, from which detonations were heard, and these were followed by the whistling or hissing sound that accompanied the fall of a black stone. The latter, which nearly buried itself in the soil, weighed seven pounds and a half, and was so burning hot that no one could touch it.—The stone that fell at Angers, June 9, 1822, was attributed to a beautiful shooting-star seen at Poitiers. Humboldt relates that this meteor had the effect of a Roman candle in a display of fireworks, and left a train in a straight line of such glowing brilliancy that the light lasted for several minutes.

AN EXTRAORDINARY METEOR.

In a letter addressed to M. A. Quételet, the permanent secretary of the Royal Academy of

Belgium, with regard to a remarkable meteor observed at Hurworth in October, 1854, Sir J. Herschel quotes the following description, which we give substantially as it appeared in the *Sheffield Times*. It was published by a person living at Hurworth, who, in company with his brother, saw the phenomenon :

"My brother and I were returning home at nine o'clock in the evening, and had just reached the end of the village, and were about to cross a meadow of considerable breadth. The sky was clear and starry, but dark. We were looking at one of the brightest constellations, when, at the very point on which our gaze was fixed, we beheld a magnificent sight. A cry of admiration and astonishment escaped us both. What we saw was a globe of fire, at least double the size of the moon when it rises. It was as red as blood, and shot out sparkling rays, which were marked in sharp outlines, as old engravings represent the rays of the sun. It drew after it a long trail of light of the most beautiful limpid golden color. The train had no resemblance to the hairy tail of a comet, but was more like a solid column, of great breadth and perfect compactness, standing out against the deep blue of the sky. In the beginning it presented the appearance of a straight line, but as it mounted the heavens, it described the curve of an arch with sparkling scintillations of great intensity, which, however, did not pass beyond the well-defined exterior line. Its direction was from northeast to southwest, and its length so enormous that, when its nucleus was disappearing under the southwestern horizon, the tail was still visible at the northeast in all its original splendor.

"When this globe of fire was immediately above us, it seemed to pause for a moment with vibrations so violent that I was afraid it would fall on us. But, the next instant, I saw that the vibration was only a whirling motion, and that it was turning rapidly on its axis, passing from a vivid fiery red to the deep red mentioned above, without, however, losing any thing of its general appearance. We continued to see it, looking as brilliant as ever, behind the trees on the other side of the village. While this globe was passing over us it seemed a little smaller than when it first appeared on the horizon, no doubt because of its great elevation, just as the sun and the moon look smaller at their meridian than when they are rising.

"As I have been, for a long time past, in the habit of watching the stars, I have seen several brilliant meteors, but never any that could bear

THE HURWORTH METEOR.

p. 214.

the least comparison to this one, whether for dimensions or for splendor and duration. Owing to its height in the air, it must have been visible at a great distance, and I hoped that it would have been seen and described by intelligent observers. As such, however, has not been the case, I have thought it my duty to furnish some details concerning a phenomenon so grând and striking."

According to Sir John Herschel's letter, this phenomenon was seen, in like manner, by many other persons, at Darlington, at Durham, and at Dundee, in Scotland:

"It is quite remarkable that, in consulting the register which records the observations made of the famous meteor that crossed England on the 18th of April, 1783, we found that it was seen at Windsor about nine o'clock, which was precisely the hour at which we saw this one, my brother having looked at his watch at the moment of its appearance. The meteor of 1783, having appeared during the twilight of a summer evening, would, no doubt, have been more generally observed than the latter phenomenon, which showed itself in a dark night at the close of autumn. But, for this very reason, the latter should have been much more brilliant than the former one, and it is to be regretted that the lateness of the hour, or rather of the season, should have prevented it from being as generally observed.

"No noise, accompanying its passage, reached us. Those who saw the enormous globe of fire, sweeping across the sky with inconceivable velocity, will never forget that magnificent and wonderful meteor. In beholding unrolled above us that splendid train of light, which covered more than half of the sombre vault of the heavens with a golden arch, we involuntarily thought of the spectacle that must be presented to the eyes of the inhabitants of Saturn by the ring that encircles that planet. The tail, near where it ended, broadened enormously; it seemed more transparent, and less compact, yet with well-defined outlines, and rounding off at the extremity. The illustration accompanying this letter was sketched with the hope of attracting general attention to an occurrence so interesting, rather than with any pretension of giving even a feeble idea of this rare and splendid phenomenon."

VELOCITY AND APPEARANCE OF BOLIDES.

The speed of these fire-balls is now calculated with considerable accuracy, as will be seen from the following extract taken from the researches of M. Heiss, the director of the Münster Observatory.

The superb bolide which he describes was seen, on the 14th of March, 1863, in Holland, Belgium, Germany, England, and France:

"Toward seven o'clock in the evening, the meteor appeared in the sky like a shooting-star; but, little by little, it enlarged until it presented an apparent surface comparable to a quarter of the moon, and a brightness that made the stars visible at the time seem pale. After having illumined the horizon with a vivid light, which different observers have described as exhibiting all the colors of the rainbow, from red to violet, the fire-ball disappeared with an explosion. In many places, sparks and a train were seen. The duration of the phenomenon was about five seconds. The trajectory, directed north and south, was inclined twenty-two degrees to the horizon, and the length of the arc—described from the point of *inflammation* to that of explosion, at about twenty-six kilometres (sixteen and three-quarter miles) above the surface of the ground—was two hundred and eighty-five kilometres (one hundred and seventy-seven, nine-hundredths miles). This indicated a speed of one hundred and sixty-three kilometres (thirty-nine, fourteen-hundredths miles) per second. Four hundred and twenty yards was the real diameter of the blazing globe, which must have been, generally, of a gaseous nature, with no solid nucleus."

It is this extreme velocity, superior to that of our globe in its orbit, which, with the resistance of the air, accounts for the appearances presented by these fire-balls. "The heat which the meteorites possess," says Sir John Herschel, in his Astronomy, "when they fall upon the soil, the igneous phenomena that accompany them, and their explosion, when they penetrate the denser layers of the atmosphere, are all sufficiently explained by the aid of physical laws. They are caused by the condensation of the air, occasioned by their enormous swiftness of translation, and by the relations that subsist between highly-rarefied air and heat." The explosion is attributed to the pressure sustained by the solid mass. Calculation shows that, at the height of eighteen kilometres, where the density of the air is ten times less than at the surface of the earth, a velocity of forty kilometres would produce a pressure of six hundred and seventy-five atmospheres. Iron might sustain this, but it would cause a stone to burst. This calculation is confirmed by actual observation: aërolites composed almost exclusively of iron come to the ground entire, but such as are of less solid consistency fall in fragments.

On the 14th of October, 1863, about three o'clock in the morning, M. J. Schmidt, director of the Athens Observatory, succeeded in following a very remarkable *bolide* with the telescope. The meteor in question appeared like a shooting-star, rather slow in movement, between the constellations of the Hare and the Dove. " It soon surpassed Sirius in splendor. Its color was a clear yellow. It passed Eridanus toward the west, shedding a light so extraordinary that all the stars were eclipsed, while the city of Athens, the country, and the sea, looked as though on fire. The Acropolis and the Parthenon stood out, a dead greenish-gray in hue, against a background of golden-green sky."

At this moment M. Schmidt, resorting to his telescope, was enabled to observe the meteor for several seconds, and note a curious phenomenon: There was not merely a single luminous body to be seen, but he discovered two brilliant bolides of a greenish-yellow, in the form of elongated drops: the larger preceded the smaller, and each left a red track, with well-defined edges. These two bodies were, moreover, followed by luminous bodies of less size and similar appearance, irregularly distributed, like sparks in the train of the bolides. At the moment of its disappearance, the meteor appeared divided into four or five fragments, of a dark red. No noise was heard either before or after the disappearance.

FALL OF AËROLITES.

We will cite, in addition, some details concerning a more recent appearance of bolides and the fall of aërolites in the south of France:

"Yesterday (May 14, 1864), at eight o'clock in the evening," writes an observer at Castillon, in the department of the Gironde, "a magnificent meteor was seen by us in the vicinity of the moon, and in an easterly course. It was visible for about five seconds, during which time it swept over an arc of more than sixty degrees. At last it burst into smaller stars and disappeared.

"The apparent size of the meteor constantly increased by progressive augmentations. A moment before disappearing, its diameter seemed equal to at least half that of the moon. At first, the light had a greenish-blue tinge; then it became white, and shone with such brilliancy that persons badly situated for a direct view of the meteor, thought they had seen the reflection of a vivid and prolonged flash of lightning."

In many places distant from each other, a loud detonation was heard, and an interval of some duration elapsed between the visible explosion of the meteor and the hearing of the noise. Three or four minutes were counted, and only two minutes correspond to a vertical distance of forty kilometres. The atmospheric layers at that height are greatly rarefied, and, in order that an explosion taking place in those regions should cause a noise of such intensity at the surface of the earth, and over a horizontal extent so considerable, we must admit that it exceeded in violence any thing known to us.

Judging by the apparent height and dimensions of the fire-ball, its diameter was estimated to be from four hundred to five hundred yards. It was then four or five times the size of the Paris cathedral. M. Laussédat calculated that its velocity was fifteen miles per second, or, in other words, about two-thirds of the rapidity of the earth in its orbit. Aërolites have been picked up near Orgeuil, in the department of Lot-et-Garonne, and in many neighboring places. M. Daubrée, who examined them, found that they resembled *terrene lignites*. "In this black mass," he says, "may be distinguished small particles of a metallic substance, of a bronzed-yellow color, the density of which allows them to be isolated by washing. Examining these little grains with a microscope, I recognized some very compact crystalline forms, but of very small dimensions. These grains, or particles, are very strongly attracted by the magnet, and possess all the physical and chemical characteristics of the magnetic pyrites discovered forty years ago in the meteoric stone of Juvinas. The meteorite of Orgeuil should be classified with the *coaly* meteors, of which the fall of three only has thus far been recorded. The surface of all the fragments was found to be fused and vitrified; however, the interior included substances which could easily be volatilized. These two circumstances, apparently contradictory, may be explained, if it be admitted that the heat undergone by the meteorites was of such brief duration that it could not penetrate the interior of the mass, the substance of which, moreover, was a bad conductor of caloric. In the case to which we are now referring, the heat must have been in some sort instantaneous, yet of considerable intensity, for it required the red-white heat of the blow-pipe to reproduce artificially the varnishy melted surface that is left by fusion. Not only is the interior part of the meteorite tender and friable, but it is reduced to impalpable powder, the moment that it comes in contact with water, and the soluble salt that serves to cement it is dissolved."

COMPOSITION OF AËROLITES.

In studying aërolites, and comparing them with other minerals, *savants* have arrived at the conclusion that they are indeed composed of the same elements (nearly a third of the known simple bodies), but that, in the method of aggregation, they are entirely different, and must be regarded as strangers to our globe. Whatever may be the date or locality of their fall, they have very evident common characteristics, and this relation is so striking that they might have been regarded as having formed part of the same rock: on the outside, a black incrustation, a glistening enamel, produced by very high temperatures, but penetrating only a few hair-breadths; and, in the interior, a singular, granulated structure, presenting some very strange features, which, when polished, might be compared to hieroglyphics. An aërolite often resembles a stone at which shot had been fired. The granulations are sometimes extremely diminutive, as in the specimen described above; sometimes, as large as millet, as peas, or even as hazelnuts. They are hard, and, when broken, exhibit crystallization. The matter in which they are incrusted is of an earthy nature, more or less consistent, and ordinarily gray. The substances that compose it are for the most part mechanically mixed, and not chemically combined. Aërolites composed almost entirely of iron are put in a class apart from the rest, so that they may be decomposed in grains. It must be remarked that this iron is in nowise oxidated; that it is, as mineralogists say, in *its native state*, and that, with the nickel, which it most usually holds in combination, stamps aërolites with a mark altogether peculiar in its way.

Stony aërolites, formed by the mixture of different mineral substances, constantly have the appearance of fragments, and they are not found in large masses, like those which are almost entirely composed of iron. There have been some enormous specimens among the last. The meteoric mass observed by Pallas, on the plains of Siberia, weighed one thousand five hundred and forty pounds. It was held in veneration by the Tartars, and regarded by them as having fallen from heaven. A mass, found in Brazil, weighed fully six tons and six-tenths. According to M. Beudant, there is a similar mass, weighing fifteen tons and eight hundred pounds, at Olimpa, in the Tucuman country, and one of fifteen and nine-tenths tons in the environs of Durango in Mexico. In the eastern part of Asia, not far from the source of the

Yellow River, there is a mass about forty feet in height, according to the statement of Abel Rémusat. The Mongols call it the *Rock of the Pole*, and say that it fell after the appearance of a meteor. The only aërolite of this character, the celestial origin of which is ascertained, fell near Agram, in Dalmatia, on the 26th of May, 1751.

The most remarkable aërolite which the mineralogical galleries of the French Museum possess, is that of Privas, in Ardèche. It fell on June 5, 1821, weighs two hundred and two and four-tenths pounds, and buried itself more than seven inches in the ground. An approximative calculation, based upon data collected since they have been observed with greater care, estimates the number of meteoric descents at about six hundred annually. The rocks of native iron, resting on the soil in different parts of the globe, and not homogeneous with the surrounding land, are also probably aërolites.

Usually, the aërolites which people have succeeded in touching at the moment of their fall, were very hot, but one was recently noted in the Punjaub that froze the hands of those who attempted to pick it up. It is easy to explain this low temperature, if we admit that these bodies have traversed the interplanetary spaces, where, according to some physiologists, the temperature descends to one hundred and forty degrees. The passage through our atmosphere heats, as we have seen, only the surface of the meteoric mass, which, in breaking, lets fall fragments of the central part, that retains its very low temperature. In metallic aërolites, the transmission of the enormous external heat is very rapid, and they often reach the earth in the condition of red-hot balls.

PERIODICAL DISPLAYS.

When the celestial origin of these meteoric bodies was, at last, recognized, it was thought that they might come from the moon, and that they were the product of its volcanoes. It was calculated that, in order to cause them to pass beyond the limit of our satellite's attraction, a force double that which projects the ball from our heaviest cannon would suffice. They would then come near enough to revolve around the earth, and sometimes be drawn to its surface. But this explanation did not account for the new appearances that we are about to mention, and which have led to a more general hypothesis. These appearances embrace the flood of meteors which illuminates the heavens at different periods of the year, and of which the displays offer a remarkable

1

SHOWER OF SHOOTING-STARS.

element of periodicity. Olmstead and Palmer have given descriptions of the enormous shower of falling-stars which they saw in America during the night between the 12th and 13th of November, 1833. The meteors fell like snow-flakes, and, in the lapse of nine hours, the number seen from one station was estimated at more than two hundred thousand. They shone with various colors; fire-balls of all dimensions were mingled with them, and in the depth of the firmament light phosphorescent traces were detected. In 1799, at the same period of the year, Humboldt had witnessed a phenomenon nearly as brilliant, at Cumana. In 1823, and again in 1832, a similar one was seen in Europe, and it was then observed regularly every year until 1842. But from that year the date of its appearance became displaced and pushed on toward the close of October. At the same time, the phenomenon had greatly diminished, and had even entirely disappeared.

Such was not the case in reference to another date, which is kept up with great precision. It is the 10th of August, or rather it covers the space from the 9th until the 11th of that month. Unquestionable documents establish the fact that the Chinese astronomers observed showers of shooting-stars more than ten centuries ago, at the same periodical date, and for a long series of years. In France, the popular tradition relative to the fiery tears of Saint Lawrence on his fête day, the 10th of August, indicates under a legendary form the periodical return of these showers of meteors. M. Herrick (Arago quoting him) states that, according to an old tradition popular in Thessaly, in the midst of the mountainous countries that surround Mount Pelion, the sky opens during the night of August 6th, the festival of the Transfiguration, and torches are visible through the orifice.

The most recent investigations show that, during the greater part of our century, the phenomenon has recurred with constant regularity, and has been visible over the entire globe.

M. Quételet, in a learned memoir on the "shooting-stars of the 10th of August period, in 1863," reproduces the following letter from Sir John Herschel:

"As for my opinion concerning these enigmatical phenomena (that is to say, so far as the question of their origin inside or outside of our atmosphere goes), I could not but admit the necessity of attributing them to a cosmic origin. Otherwise, I can see no explanation, in the least degree admissible in any other quarter, of the persistence from year to year of the same point of radiation in contrast with others, nor of the regular recurrence on the same day of the year (August 10th), unless by the earth meeting with a belt of 'something' revolving around the sun. Without doubt this explanation leaves something yet to be explained, but it satisfies the two grand conditions of the problem, and these two grand conditions are the most striking. As to their great elevation above the earth, it leads us to *suspect* the existence of a kind of atmosphere higher up than the aërial atmosphere, lighter, and, so to speak, more *igneous* than our own."

M. Quételet's important work, entitled "Physique du Globe," published in 1861, designates these two atmospheric strata of different consistency as the *movable atmosphere*, subject to variations of all kinds, and the *immovable atmosphere*, of very feeble density, which remains in a condition of relative stability, or fixedness. "This upper atmosphere, favorable to the combustion and to the brilliance of the shooting-stars, would not necessarily be of the same nature and the same composition as the lower atmosphere in which we live."

M. Quételet also calls attention to the fact, that the very existence of the shooting-stars naturally leads to the admission that the height of the atmosphere must be at least three or four times what it is now supposed to be.

OBSCURATION OF THE SUN.

"The sun's disk," says Arago, in his "Popular Astronomy," under the head of Cosmic Meteors, "is sometimes obscured for a few moments, and its light becomes enfeebled to such a degree that the stars may be seen at noonday. Humboldt recalls the circumstance that a phenomenon of this kind, which could not be ascribed either to fog or to volcanic cinders, took place in 1547, about the time of the disastrous battle of Mühlberg, and lasted three days. Kepler was disposed to trace the cause of it to the interposition of a *materia cometica*, or such matter as composes the train of comets, or to a black cloud which sooty emanations from the sun had contributed to form. Chladni and Schnurrer attributed it to the passage of meteoric masses over the disk of the sun, like the phenomena of this kind that occurred in 1090 and 1208, although they were of shorter duration, the first one lasting three and the second six hours only.

"Messier relates that, on the 17th of June, 1777, about noon, he saw a prodigious number of black globules pass before the sun. Did not these

THE BELT OF METEORITES. 231

globules form part of one of the rings of asteroids of which all observations of cosmic meteors tend to make us admit the existence? Two other obscurations of the sun—that in the beginning of February, 1106, and that of May 12, 1706, during which, about ten o'clock in the morning, the darkness became such that the bats began to fly about—seem likewise inexplicable by any other theory."

THE BELT OF METEORITES.

According to M. Faye, the meteoric display of November, and that of several other months, may be connected in the following manner with the one seen in August: The earth, in its passage through the belt of unknown bodies revolving around the sun, carries along with it, by its power of attraction, a great number of those bodies, which thenceforth become her veritable satellites. This collection burns in the atmosphere, in the course of the year, and precipitates itself upon our planet's surface. During their circulation in our orbit some of these meteorites may pass singly, like those that are seen every evening. Others, assembled in different groups, approach or recede, according to their position in the orbit that they follow, and occasion the displays of November and other times whose periodicity is kept up during only a limited number of years. This hypothesis would explain the appearance of swarms of satellites seen in a single quarter of the heavens.

The ingenious opinions which we have just summed up may enable the reader to judge of the lively interest that attaches, at the present time, to what M. Faye calls " the mystery of the shooting-stars." Scarcely the first veil that enshrouded it has yet fallen, indeed; but observers multiply in number and combine their efforts, and learned men are uniting their labors, sustained by the profound feeling that inspired the following pages from the pen of Humboldt:

"To see motion rise suddenly in the midst of the calm of night, and for a moment disturb the tranquil radiance of the starry vault; to follow with the eye the meteor which, in falling, traces its luminous trajectory athwart the firmament—is not this to have one's thoughts ascend, straightway, to those infinite spaces which are filled everywhere with matter, and everywhere vivified with movement? Of what consequence is the diminutive size of these meteors in a system where, along with the enormous volume of the sun, one finds atoms as small as Ceres, or as the first satellite of the planet Saturn? What matters their sudden disappearance when a phenomenon of another order, the extinction of those stars that shone all at once in Cassiopeia, in the Swan, and in Serpentarius, has already forced us to admit that there may exist in the celestial spaces other stars than those that we always see there? We know the fact, now, that shooting-stars are aggregations of matter, veritable asteroids, that circulate around the sun, which, like comets, sweep across the orbits of the larger planets, and shine near our atmosphere, or, at least, in its highest strata.

"Isolated upon our planet from all parts of the creation which the limits of our atmosphere do not embrace, we are not in communication with the celestial bodies, excepting by the rays of heat and light, and by that mysterious attraction which those distant masses exert upon our globe, our seas, and even the beds of air that surround us. But, if aërolites and shooting-stars be really planetary asteroids, the method of communication changes: it becomes more direct, and, in some sort, assumes a material shape. In fact, we no longer have to deal with those far remote bodies, the action of which, upon the earth, is limited to the production of luminous or calorific vibrations, or motions in accordance with the laws of a reciprocal attraction of gravitation. We now have before our contemplation material bodies, which, abandoning the celestial spaces, traverse our atmosphere, and dash against the earth, and thenceforth form a portion of it. Such is the only cosmical event that can put our planet in contact with the other parts of the universe. Accustomed as we are to know things placed outside of our globe only through the medium of measurement, calculation, and reasoning, we are now surprised at being able to touch them, weigh them, and analyze them. It is thus that science brings the secret springs of the imagination and the living forces of the mind into play in our souls, while the vulgar throng behold in these phenomena but sparks that flash up and then die out, and in these black stones, that fall with a crash from the bosom of the clouds, nothing but the coarse product of some convulsion of Nature."

CHAPTER X.

DUST IN THE ATMOSPHERE.—DRY FOGS.

Cosmic Dust.—Volcanic Ashes.—The Sands of the Deserts.—The Red Mists of Cape Verde.—Showers of Manure.—Dry Fogs.

COSMIC DUST.

A COSMIC origin must be assigned to a great deal of the dust that falls from the atmosphere. Not only have aërolites of very slight consistency been picked up, but many *savants* think that the appearance of *bolides* is often due to bodies of dusty consistency traversing the celestial spaces. This hypothesis was announced, in 1849, by M. Heiss, in his work upon periodical shooting-stars. "It is easily understood," says M. Haidinger, in an interesting memoir, " that agglomerations of dusty matter, collected in a globular form, and passing through the upper strata of the atmosphere, first excite, in their totality, certain luminous phenomena. But they must soon be resolved again into dust, leaving nothing in existence that could determine a development of light. We would here recall the fact that, according to M. Julius Schmidt, the most luminous meteors seem to blaze up at more considerable heights, while those of less intense brightness belong to less elevated regions. The different modes of the diffusion of their light may be attributed to the greater or less volume of the particles. The smallest grains of dust emit light so soon as they reach the upper strata, and die out just as quickly, because, after a short course, they are dispersed by the resistance of the atmosphere. The less diffused particles make a longer run, but they also die out, generally at considerable heights."

The great meteors that descend to the lower strata, and are seen to have a rotary movement, and disappear without causing a fall of aërolites, may be considered as relatively voluminous agglomerations of dusty matter. They frequently leave behind them luminous trains that last for some time. Admiral Krusenstern, in his voyage around the world, saw the broad track of a *bolide* shining for more than an hour, without seeming to change place to any perceptible degree. We have mentioned the clouds that are seen during the daytime in the track of meteors. Mr.

B. V. Marsh, describing the one that appeared on the 15th of November, 1859, in a part of America, says that it left a column of smoke about a thousand feet in diameter, the base of which was at an elevation of nearly eight thousand. These appearances can be explained only by supposing the presence of immense masses of dusty matter.

M. von Reichenbach, who has paid much attention to aërolites, has published some remarkable studies in reference to their relations with comets, which he considers as being composed of the same material reduced to very minute particles widely separated from each other. The condensation of these clouds of cosmic dust at different degrees, seemed to him to explain the granulated appearance observed in meteoric stones, and even in masses of iron which he succeeded in separating into globules.

The fall of dust, the matter of which was identical with that of aërolites, has been ascertained, beyond a doubt, by recent chemical analysis, as well as by quite a number of historical accounts. Pliny affirms that "a fire was seen to fall from heaven in a shower of blood." This fire must have been the light emanating from a *bolide*, and the blood a red dust mixed with the rain. In Procopius, there is mention made of a great fall of black dust in the environs of Constantinople, in the year 472; it must have accompanied a luminous meteor, since, according to the historian, "the heavens seemed on fire."

Arago has compiled many similar facts in his "Popular Astronomy." He mentions the fall of red and blackish matter that took place at Verde, in Hanover, and was accompanied by a globe of fire and violent detonations. This matter burned the wood-work upon which it fell. On March 14, 1813, red dust and red snow fell in Calabria, Tuscany, and Friuli, and, at the same time, a great noise, and the falling of stones, were heard at Cutro. Sementini found, in several specimens of this dust, the ordinary chemical composition of aërolites.

In November, 1819, a black rain and snow fell at Montreal, and in the northern part of the United States. This fall was accompanied by an extraordinary darkening of the sky, shocks similar to those felt during an earthquake, detonations, and very powerful flashes of lightning. Some persons have attributed these phenomena to the conflagration of forests, but the noise, the shocks, and all the circumstances, go to show that it was a real meteor.

The American sea-captain Callam reports a

curious observation made by him. His ship was in the Indian Ocean, to the southward of Java, when a shower of very small stones fell suddenly on the deck, without the occurrence of any other phenomenon to explain this odd circumstance. He picked up several fragments, and Commander Maury, to whom he gave them on his return to America, sent them to M. Ehrenberg, who, by the aid of a powerful microscope, ascertained that the matter of these fragments had originally been liquid, but had been solidified during its descent. It offered complete resemblance to the residue resulting from the combustion of a steel wire burned in a flask full of oxygen; and this leads us to infer that the fragments were drops of water falling from the incandescent surface of an aërolite which had passed above the ship.

VOLCANIC ASHES.

Clouds of dust rise from the bosom of the earth, also, that frequently spread through a great breadth of atmosphere. These are the volcanic ashes, which, sometimes scattered by the winds, and sometimes falling in dense showers on the soil, bury whole cities beneath them. The following narrative of the most memorable of these catastrophes will give an idea of the phenomenon:

"In 79, under the Emperor Titus, Pliny the naturalist was in command of the Roman fleet, near Cape Misenum, westward of Naples. His sister, the mother of Pliny the Younger, drew his attention one evening to a cloud of extraordinary size and shape. This cloud, after rising in a vertical column, expanded at the top and assumed the appearance of a spreading pine-tree. Pliny ordered out a boat and went rapidly toward Vesuvius, from which, as was soon perceived, this cloud, or rather this smoke, ascended. The dense shower of cinders, pumice-stone, and fragments of rock, hurled from the crater, was already terrifying the neighboring country-people, but the naturalist advanced boldly to the scene of danger. Near Stabia, he passed the night in a villa, and, being much fatigued, slept so profoundly that his breathing could be heard outside. When he awoke, it was only with some difficulty that he could leave the house, the cinders having nearly choked up the doorway. At the break of day, which the eruption rendered nearly as dark as night, he tried to advance nearer to the mountain, in order to observe the phenomenon. The flames and sulphurous vapors, that made everybody else recoil, only stimulated his ardent courage. But, soon afterward, he was seen striving to rise from the spot where he had sat down for a moment, and then suddenly fall, struck with apoplexy or suffocated by the fumes."

It may be remembered that during this violent eruption the cities of Pompeii, Stabia, and Herculaneum, disappeared, the first two under a mass of cinders and scoriæ, and the latter beneath the lava. They remained thus buried for seventeen hundred years, and their exact site was no longer remembered, when, by accident, they were again discovered."

Captain Basil Hall reports the following:— "On the 1st of May, 1812, after some violent detonations, that terrified the inhabitants of Barbadoes, a black cloud was descried, seaward, upon the northern horizon. Ere long, it covered the whole sky, which had just been emerging from the shadows of morning twilight. At length, the darkness became such that it was impossible, indoors, to tell where the windows were, while, in the open air, many persons could not see either the trees near which they were passing; the outlines of the neighboring houses, or even white handkerchiefs placed a few inches from their eyes. This phenomenon was occasioned by the fall of an enormous quantity of volcanic dust issuing from a crater on the Isle of St. Vincent, and containing, according to the analysis made by Dr. Thompson, ninety-one parts of silex and aluminum, eight of calcareous matter, and one of oxide of iron. This new kind of rain, and the profound darkness it occasioned, did not cease entirely until between noon and one o'clock; but, several times during the morning, there were noticed, by the aid of a lantern, showers, so to speak, in which the dust fell in greater abundance. Trees whose wood was flexible bent beneath the burden, and the noise that the branches of other trees made in breaking contrasted in a very striking manner with the calmness of the atmosphere. The sugar-canes were completely beaten down, and the whole island was covered with a bed of greenish ashes an inch in depth."

The Isle of St. Vincent is situated about one hundred and six miles to the west of Barbadoes, and Arago inferred, from the passage of volcanic ashes to such a distance, that there is an upper current blowing in a direction counter to the trade-winds, which in these regions, and particularly during the months of April and May, blow uniformly from the eastward with a slight deviation to the north. We must, then, admit that the volcano on St. Vincent had hurled the immense quantity of ashes, which fell upon Barbadoes and the adjacent seas, to a height where not only the trade-winds ceased to be felt, but even where a current diametrically the reverse of them prevailed.

When dispersed by the winds, volcanic ashes sometimes travel very great distances. Those that issued from Vesuvius were found at Constantinople. In the formidable eruption of Tomboro, a volcano of the island of Sumbawa, which took place in April, 1815, the ashes went as far as Java, Macassar, and Batavia. They even fell at Bencoolen, in Sumatra, more than nine hundred and thirty-one miles distant.

THE DESERT SANDS.

On the deserts, the winds carry great masses of sand, which sometimes cause terrible catastrophes. The soil is composed of light sand, which the storm tosses as it does the billows of the sea. Enormous whirlwinds bury whole caravans, and frequently it is by the bones found in the sandy beds that the way across these vast solitudes is recognized.

One characteristic feature of our globe is the line of deserts that traverses Africa and Asia, forming a zone of four hundred leagues in diameter at some points, with a total length of nearly three thousand leagues from the Senegal to the Nile, and from Arabia to Mongolia. In certain localities of Sahara, and in the Desert of Cobi, the bottom of ancient seas has been distinctly recognized; and one may readily conceive of an epoch when the series of these internal sheets of water, the Mediterranean, the Black Sea, the Caspian, the Aral, and all the lakes of the steppes as far as Lake Baikal, was repeated in a more southern but parallel region more exposed to drought.

"This prolongation of continuity in the deserts," says Jean Reynaud, developing this hypothesis, "might be very readily explained by one of the great laws of the atmosphere, viz.: the habitual movement of the air from west to east in the temperate zones. Supposing separate and distinct aggregations of sand to have existed originally, and to have been arranged like the present great desert, along a line not very widely diverging from the parallel of the equator, the sand being constantly thrown toward the east by the wind, would, at length, necessarily have formed along the whole line, commencing at its point of departure, lengthened sandy trains joining the other trains behind it, and thus have united all the primitive deserts in one single waste. This displacement of the deserts, this continual extension of their limits toward the east, in the temperate zones, at least, is an ascertained fact. Nature has not fixed the sand as she has the sea. God did not say to the desert when He created it, 'Thus far shalt thou go, and no farther.' It is not Egypt, at all events, that would contradict our assertion. The wind drives the sand of Sahara over that country, and has already scattered enough upon it to almost entirely cover the upper tracts of the valley of the Nile. In a few centuries more, Upper Egypt will be completely buried; the sands will accumulate at the foot of the mountains that separate the region in question from the Red Sea, until, at length attaining their level, they may continue their onward march, and extend over Arabia the continuous mantle of the desert.

"The districts of the Thebaid, once the most densely-peopled and most flourishing on earth, now belong to the sandy waste. The temples rear their desolate capitals above the sand as though above the waters of a deluge; and the sphinxes, like those fossil creatures of the antediluvian world, of which no traces are now discovered, excepting in the bosom of the subterranean strata, repose peacefully in its depths."

To this moving picture of the progressive invasion of the deserts, Jean Reynaud adds the following considerations: "Will the trip across these inhospitable solitudes ever become more prompt and easy than it is now? Has the industry of civilized nations any thing to add to what the experience of the nomadic tribes who haunt the desert, has invented for this purpose? In my mind, the reply to this question is not doubtful, so great does the scope of human power appear to me; but, at the same time, I recognize the fact that such a task is beyond its strength. We have subjected the ocean by means of steam, we may subdue the mountains when we will by the aid of inclined railroads, but how shall we ever make the untamable elements of the desert submit? It is a rude problem to solve. Its solution assuredly cannot be directly approached, and, besides, the time has not yet come. But it suffices to state the question, in order to catch a glimpse, at once, of the full majesty of the desert. A force which has broken down so many other barriers has not even a hold on this one. All that we have to go upon, in attempting to speak with certainty on this subject, for the honor of man, is, that the engineer now knows how to fix and confine the moving sands by covering their edges with sufficient plantations of trees; that the agriculturist, by the aid of irrigation, succeeds little by little in cultivating and fertilizing the most arid waste; and finally, that, in countries the most remote from river-courses, the miner can, like Moses in the desert, by striking the rocks with his iron rod, make springs leap from them, and thus give birth, in plains the most destitute of all the gifts of Nature, to verdant oases. But from these attempts, made on a small scale in some districts, to the general cultivation of Sahara, and to the establishment of well-made roads across a grassy surface, where all now is sand, there is a lapse of time to come as prolonged as the imagination can conceive."

Let us here add that the recent discovery of an immense watery deposit extending under the Algerian part of Sahara, admits the hope of at least a slow transformation. At every spot where the subterranean sheet bursts forth, forests of palm-trees, that form the oases, quickly spring up. The oasis of Ouargla, which possesses a great number of Artesian wells, counts as many as one hundred and fifty thousand palm-trees, that, according to the Arab saying, live with "their feet in the water, and their heads in the fire." These still favor the cultivation of the ground, which is not possible excepting beneath their sheltering shade.

Navigators, in following the coast of Africa, often encounter winds to which their burning heat, an extreme dryness, and the presence of sand, give a peculiar character, that must be attributed to their passing over the desert. These winds are designated according to locality, as the *simoom*, the *sirocco*, the *khamsin*, the *harmattan*, etc. During the continuance of the *simoom*, which often blows in a whirlwind, a temperature of fifty degrees has been noted in the shade. The *sirocco* reaches the coasts of Italy, and carries the sand along with it. The *khamsin*, which is of very elevated temperature, owes it name, meaning *fifty*, to its long duration. It precedes and follows the equinox for twenty-five days. The *harmattan* blows upon the coast of Guinea, and is always accompanied by a peculiar kind of fog. "This fog," says Arago, "is so dense as to afford passage to but few rays of the sun at noonday, and always rises when the *harmattan* is blowing. The particles of which it is formed deposit themselves on the sod, on the leaves of the trees, and on the skin of the negroes, in such fashion that every thing for the time being looks white. The nature of these particles is unknown. All that we do know about them is, that the wind carries them but a very little distance out upon the ocean away from the coasts. Only one league at sea the fog is much attenuated, and at three leagues there is not a trace of it to be seen, although the *harmattan* makes itself felt there in full force."

THE RED FOGS AT CAPE VERDE.

M. Ehrenberg believes that the name of *dark* or *gloomy* sea, given to the Atlantic by the ancients, took its rise in the phenomenon observed after the mariner has issued forth from the Straits of Gibraltar and is drawing near to the waters by Cape Verde. At the approach of the equinoxes, and during an interval that varies from thirty to forty days, there falls a very fine red powder that obscures the atmosphere and deposits itself upon the rigging of vessels. This shower of dust, known also as the red fog, extends over a sea-surface of more than a million of square miles.

Showers of red dust have been frequently noted, also, at different points on the Mediterranean, and in Europe and Western Asia, but at irregular epochs. Near Lyons, for instance, in 1846, there fell a quantity, estimated in all at seven thousand two hundred quintals, on a surface of four hundred square miles. This dust is not composed of sand and clay alone, but also of organic substances and infusoria, which a powerful microscope renders quite visible. A sort of worm, which, along with the clay, gives color to the mixture, is so small that it requires nearly two millions of these animalcula to fill the space of a cubic inch. One thing especially remarkable is, that, in the many specimens examined by M. Ehrenberg, and collected on the Atlantic as well as in Europe, Asia Minor, and Syria, the same species have always been found. The *savant* in question has prepared a chart on which all the places where this dust has fallen are marked. He admits that the showers of blood mentioned in history may have been confounded with this phenomenon, since the fluid in question might well be represented by the red substance above mentioned, when the latter is moistened with water, and such an explanation of the legendary fact is too obvious to be rejected.

The interesting question of the origin of these peculiar kinds of dust then occupied his attention, and led him to analyze a great many specimens of the soil collected in different parts of Africa and South America. The result showed that nowhere on the first-named continent could species of infusoria be found the same as those discovered in the dust, while on the second they were met with near the Orinoco and Amazon Rivers.

This circumstance very forcibly struck the attention of Commander Maury, who saw that these dust-falls may serve to mark the extent of the circuit made by the aërial currents, just as bottles thrown into the sea by mariners mark the sweep of the ocean-currents.

The periodicity indicated by the appearance of this dust at Cape Verde has relation, according to Maury, to the movement of oscillation north and south of the zone of equatorial calms, a movement that carries the rainy season from point to point over the surface of America. "At the period of the spring equinox," he says, "the valley of the lower Orinoco is in its dry season; the marshes and plains in that region are converted into arid deserts; the water has, so to speak, disappeared, and the trade-winds can very readily bear away with them the dust that whirls about on these parched savannas. Six months later, at the autumnal equinox, the relative position of the zones of calm and of the trade-winds has changed. It is the greater part of the valley of the Amazon which becomes a prey to drought and which in its turn furnishes to the heavy breezes of that period of the year the organic dust that we find in the other hemisphere."

Humboldt gives us an easy comprehension of

how the dust is carried up from those burning plains: "When, under a vertical sun and a cloudless sky, the grassy carpet is scorched to a cinder and reduced to dust, the baked soil cracks open as though it had been split by violent shocks of earthquake. Should opposite currents of air meet each other midway at this moment, and by their conflicting action produce a gyrating movement, the plain presents a strange spectacle to the observer. The sand rises like a conical cloud, the point of which scores the ground, in the midst of the whirlwind, which is highly charged with electricity. It might be mistaken for one of those howling tornadoes so dreaded by the experienced seaman. The vault of the heavens, which seems lower down than usual, reflects only a dull and opaline light over the plain. Suddenly, the horizon seems to draw closer and space contracts. Suspended in the cloudy atmosphere, the red, hot dust still augments the suffocating temperature of the air; and, instead of refreshing coolness, the east wind, sweeping over the burning soil, only brings a more blazing heat."

SHOWERS OF MANURE.

We have still to mention certain kinds of dust that are floating continually around us, and which the luminous ray causes to appear to us, in any dark space, in whirlwinds of sparkling particles.

There mingle in the dust of our streets and roads some detached remains of every thing we use—the tiny atoms of the smoke that rises from our hearths, as well as the floating molecules that escape in the decomposition of organic bodies. These materials are of great value, as learned agriculturalists have indicated. " Perhaps," says M. Barral, "it would be correct to say, that the air remaining in a condition of purity equal to that which is sometimes attained in our laboratories, would strike the earth with barrenness. Perhaps, too, it is necessary for the maintenance of life on our planet, that a host of impurities should be incessantly carried hither and thither, by the winds and the storms, from the places where they are produced to regions where germs are waiting to be fructified."

A great number of salts (for instance, marine salt), that are adapted to the provision of elements necessary to vegetation, exist in rain-water, and consequently in the atmosphere. Dalton found one hundred and thirty-seven milligrammes of chloride of sodium (or marine salt) per litre near Manchester, and M. Barral has ascertained that there are four milligrammes in the rain-water of

Paris. As we retire from the sea, the proportion of salt diminishes, and every thing leads us to infer that this substance is raised from the billows of the ocean by the great winds, and borne toward the interior. Salt-rains are often mentioned in works on meteorology, and Pliny cites several instances. Sometimes there have been found, with the salt, the iodine and bromine that accompany it in the brine of the deep.

Particles of phosphoric matter also are often detected in the air. They have been carried up, no doubt, in the form of dust, from those parts of the globe's surface where the phosphate of lime is abundant. This dust, descending along with the rain, contributes powerfully to the fertility of the soil. Each crop of grain withdrawing seventeen and a half pounds of phosphorus per acre from the soil, and the supply yielded by the atmosphere being much less, we may readily comprehend why races who, like the Arabs, never manure their lands, are obliged, after having drawn some scanty products from them, to abandon them for several years, until the soil shall have reacquired the elements necessary for a new crop. The sea, which in certain circumstances, and particularly during tempests, becomes illuminated with the phosphorescent coruscations due

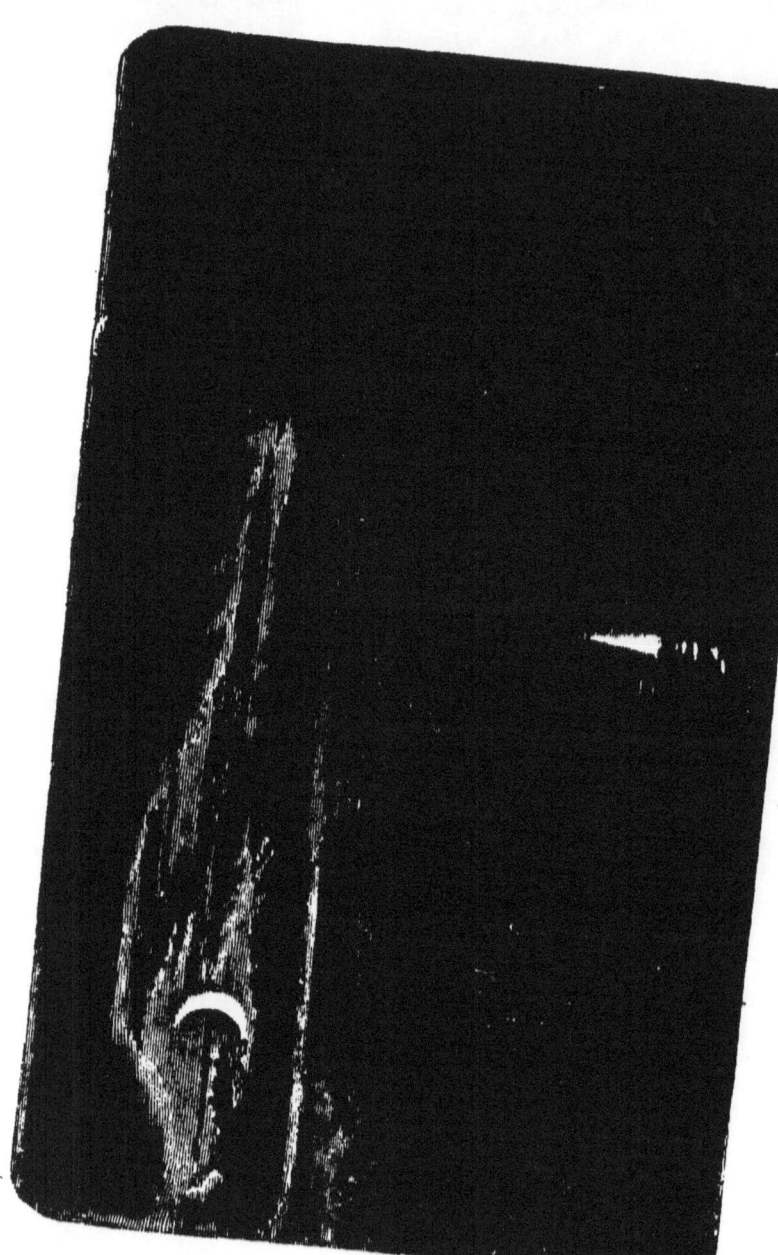

A WILL-O'-THE-WISP.

p. 253.

to the presence of innumerable animacules, must also contribute to the diffusion of phosphorus. This substance likewise comes from the subterranean putrefaction of animal matter, and disperses itself in the atmosphere, above swamps and marshes, by means of those mysterious Jack-o'-lanterns, or Will-o'-the-wisps, that have given rise to so many superstitious stories.

DRY FOGS.

We mention, along with atmospheric dust, the phenomena known as *dry fogs*, due to matter of great tenuity, but not aqueous, suspended in the atmosphere, the clearness of which they overcloud. Humboldt, when on the summit of the Silla, found himself enveloped in a dense cloud that concealed the nearest objects from his view, without his clothing being dampened in the least degree. At the same time, the hygrometer marked the highest degree of dryness.

In Switzerland, the name of *hâle* is given to a sort of smoke that accompanies the north wind during the summer, and extends around the horizon, shutting out the Alps from view. It is sometimes gray, sometimes red or russet-colored, and the sun when seen through it has a sombre, reddened hue. The *callina* is a similar exhalation in Spain, which gives the sky a leaden or livid tinge.

In the north of Germany, certain dry fogs are but real smoke produced in the fields by the combustion of turf and other vegetable matter. Broad surfaces sometimes take fire spontaneously in the peat-bogs, and the quantity of combustible material consumed often amounts to millions of pounds. It has been noted that the wind always blows from the direction of the turf-beds when there is a dry fog. "The dense fog of 1834 came," says Kaemtz, "from the combustion of the peat-beds, and from the many fires that marked the year. When it was noticed in the Hartz Mountains, toward the end of May, there were fires in the peat-beds in the neighborhood of Bâsle and Orleans. Thus, to mention one particular case, the peat-beds of Dachau, in Bavaria, burned to a depth of more than nine feet, and the fire propagated itself beneath ditches full of water. In the environs of Münster, and in Hanover, many peat-beds were consumed. Later, in July, there were terrible conflagrations in the forests and turf-pits near Berlin, in Silesia, in Sweden, and in Russia, and the drought favored the propagation of these fires and the drifting of the smoke."

M. le Verrier has given a description of a

singular cloud which is noticed daily at Paris. It comes from the smoke of the forges situated in the direction of the Maison Blanche: "The spectacle," says he, "is really curious to see. From the top of the chimney issues a cone as black as ink. This cone spreads open, little by little, gains distance over the city of Paris, and passes beyond it, sometimes to the north and sometimes to the south of the Observatory. When it passes to the northward, we follow it with our gaze as far as Gentilly. No sunshine falls at that moment on a large part of Paris. At least such is what the inhabitants think; the sun is really hidden by the smoke of these forges, while to the northward it is brilliant."

Sometimes immense swarms of insects have presented the appearance of a collection of clouds: "On Tuesday, the 7th of September, in very calm weather, workmen employed in replanting a part of the Espérou Mountain witnessed an extraordinary phenomenon, one unexampled, in fact, in those regions. At two o'clock in the afternoon, a dull and monotonous noise, almost analogous to that produced by a distant thunder-storm, fixed their attention upon a dense mist that was sweeping over a small hill about six miles in advance of them. As the air was very calm, they were astonished at this humming sound, and their first idea was of a fire in the direction of Espérou; but, determined to ascertain the real reason of so intense a mist, they were no little surprised when, as they moved toward it, they discovered that it was an immense column of gnats, the length of the cloud being some five thousand feet, with a perpendicular depth of from one hundred to two hundred feet. This column of insects was moving from east to west. An eye-witness, a forest-keeper who was superintending the workmen in the woodland, has furnished us these particulars."

An extraordinary dry fog extended, in 1783, over the whole surface of Europe, and a part of Asia. Its density was such that, in some places, objects less than a mile distant could not be distinguished, and people could look at the noonday sun without being dazzled. This phenomenon was first remarked at Copenhagen on the 9th of May, after a succession of fine days. At other places it was preceded by wind and rain. It was seen, on the 6th of June, at La Rochelle; at Dijon on the 14th, and on the 16th at Manheim and at Rome. It appeared on the 19th in the Netherlands; on the 22d, in Norway; on the 23d, on the Saint Gothard and in Hungary; toward the close of June, in Syria; and by the 1st of

DRY FOGS. 259

July on the tops of the Altai Mountains. Its duration varied at different places; and it was interrupted, here and there, by fine days. This fog had one remarkable peculiarity during the nighttime: it was phosphorescent, and the light it yielded was sufficient to read by.

A great many conjectures have been offered as to the cause of this phenomenon. Van Swinden and Toaldo think it attributable to the earthquakes and volcanic eruptions which in that same year disturbed Calabria and Iceland. From the month of February until the end of March, there were terrible commotions of the earth's surface in Calabria; mountains were shattered, an immense number of chasms opened and emitted smoke, and more than one hundred thousand human beings perished under the ruins of the fallen cities.

The eruptions commenced in Iceland on the 1st of June. Seventeen villages were swallowed up, and the lava of Hecla consumed a great quantity of vegetable matter. There were also many turf-beds in combustion throughout Europe. But none of these explanations sufficed. Franklin, at last, put forward an hypothesis that probably comes near to the truth. According to his idea, an immense fiery meteor had been burning in the upper regions of the atmosphere, and

13

the strange fog was due to a vapor of cosmic origin.

A similar phenomenon was observed in the month of August, 1831, in a part of Europe, upon the north coast of Africa, and in the United States. It diminished the light of day, and, in the night-time, diffused a phosphorescent radiance. No comet having been discovered at the epochs when these dry mists appeared, they could not be considered the product of the cometary vapors that the earth, according to Arago, has to traverse several times in the course of a century, and which must be the origin of the atmospheric phenomena that are sometimes visible, but more frequently pass unperceived, owing to the excessive tenuity of the matter that composes the tails of comets.

CHAPTER XI.

PROGNOSTICS OF THE WEATHER.

Progress of Meteorology. — Foretelling the Weather. — Orpheus, Homer, Hesiod, Virgil.—Prognostics furnished by Animals.—Prognostics from Plants, and from the State of the Sky.—Characters of the Seasons and of Future Years.—Shooting-Stars.—Influence of the Moon.

THE PROGRESS OF METEOROLOGY.

HIPPOCRATES, in his "Treatise on Atmospheres, Waters, and Places," and Aristotle, in his "Meteorologics," submitted the observation of atmospheric phenomena to experimental methods, and collated the first elements of a positive meteorology. The progress of science, notwithstanding the living impulse given by these two great minds, and in spite of the labors of Theophrastus, Pliny, and Seneca, was very slow until the middle ages, when the discoveries of Avicenna, of Albert le Grand, and Roger Bacon, caused it to take a new step in advance. But it is to the remarkable progress of the physical sciences, to Galileo, Porta, Descartes, Pascal, Huygens, and Mariotte, that meteorology owes the discoveries that have secured its development.

Among the learned men whose labors have, more recently, given a powerful flight to this most important branch of science, we may mention Humboldt and Maury, to whom we are indebted for the increased number of observations which, on land and sea, are now gathering so much precious information. It is also to their persevering initiative that we owe the large developments through which meteorology is now entering the path of practical usefulness, and, by its numerous applications to agriculture, navigation, public health, geology, etc., enhancing the universal interest its researches have always awakened.

If we bring together the superstitious notions of the past, and the teachings of contemporaneous science, we see that it is to the love of the marvellous, to our common predilection for the unknown, as much as to our primitive ignorance, that we must attribute the appeal to the supernatural made by the ancients upon nearly all occasions when they tried to account for atmospheric and terrestrial phenomena. But this tendency, which, even through so many errors, has after all guided us toward the truth, still exists in us, and we must reflect that it will never cease to intervene in our moral and intellectual progress. Directed, in our day, toward regions less obscure, toward truths more luminous and imposing, it will lead us to a higher interpretation of Divine management, and a more exact recognition of the fundamental laws the sway of which beneficently maintains "order in the universe and magnificence in order," as Humboldt has grandly said in his "Cosmos."

Notwithstanding the favorable direction imparted to meteorology by the labors of several celebrated *savants*, this science is still far from approaching the perfection of the other natural sciences. It is made up of multiple and variable phenomena, which are further complicated by a host of circumstances, from the influence of which it is impossible to separate them, and which are modified to an endless extent by climate, local arrangement, the configuration of places and sites, and the nature, the elevation, or the depression of the soil. Thus, it is only by multiplying our observations, by repeating them incessantly in different places, that we can reach the point where we can shape them into general laws, of which we may catch a glimpse in the general totality of the phenomena, but whose application escapes us under particular circumstances. Should we ever succeed in reducing the phenomena of meteorology to a small number of fundamental laws, we may, perhaps, some day get far enough on to foretell the intensity of the seasons with a certain degree of probability. Without mentioning all the advantages that would result from this, who, we may ask, would question the importance of information that would direct the cultivator how to combine his operations in accordance with the weather that would favor or retard them? But man is far from having attained such a degree of perfection as this. Nevertheless, we should not despair of yet accomplishing it. Who will venture to lay down limits to science? The human mind has already unveiled enough of Nature's secrets to let us hope that we may surprise a few more of them.

This correct appreciation of the services that meteorology is called upon to render, and of the necessity of the numerous observations which alone can give it a secure foundation, points out at once the end to be reached, and the means of reaching it. But while, for most of the other sciences, the observations to be collected are nearly always either beyond our reach, or surrounded by difficulties that confine them within the circle of a few learned men, in meteorology, on the contrary, any one may, by bringing to bear a little perseverance, acquire knowledge enough to recognize the weather-signs to a useful degree.

ORPHEUS, HOMER, HESIOD, VIRGIL.

From the first, man has found himself subjected, either directly or indirectly, to the influence of atmospheric phenomena. Exposed to the inclemencies of the weather, he not merely had to seek shelter in a substantial dwelling, but to direct his attention to the work of discovering beforehand the perturbations that he might subsequently have to endure.

The connection between these disturbances of the air, the variableness of the seasons, and the production of the fruits of the earth, was, moreover, narrowly bound up with his material well-being; and we can readily understand the gratitude of the original tribes toward those men whose intelligence, loftier, more active, more patient, and more enlightened, than their own, was enabled to seize the link between certain phenomena and the appearance of premonitory signs. The first priests, the first legislators, were also in the days of antiquity the first meteorologists. We find traces of their teachings, mingled with the strangest superstitions, in the primitive fragments attributed to Orpheus, in the poems of Homer, Hesiod, and Virgil.

Two hymns of Orpheus invoke the favoring breezes and the beneficent rains that fertilize the soil:

THE CLOUDS.

"Aërial clouds, O wanderers of heaven, generators of all the fruits! ye who hold in your bosoms the treasures of the rain; ye who traverse the world, driven by the breath of the winds; thunder-striking, flaming, reëchoing clouds, that, turn by turn, spread through the air a gentle murmur or the howl of tempests, I now implore ye to pour out upon the earth the favoring rains that fructify the buds and germs!"

THE SEASONS.

"Seasons, darling daughters of Jove and of Themis, the most fruitful goddess of all! ye who load us with benefits, O richly verdant, blossoming, pure, delicious seasons—seasons with varied mingling colors, shedding abroad a fragrant breath —ever-changing seasons, accept our pious offerings, and send us the aid of the favoring winds that make the harvests ripen!"

Homer, in the "Odyssey," and Hesiod, in his

"Works and Days," point out the first meteorological observations of seamen and farmers, the periods of each season that should be preferred, in order to conduct the tillage of the ground or avoid the dangers of navigation with success. These periods correspond with the courses of the stars, and of the principal constellations, Arcturus, the Pleiades, Orion, and Sirius, which alternately rise and disappear, marking the advance of the seasons in the starry heavens. Thus the "moist Pleiades," which, toward autumn, reascend our horizon at the beginning of night, announce the return of the rains. Arcturus, which brings back "spring with its white flowers," rises in April and presides over the first labors of the new season. Orion and Sirius light up the stormy skies of the long nights in winter, when the frost strips the fields, and when the unchained tempests detain the mariner in port.

Virgil, who has summed up in his "Georgics" the whole meteorological science of his epoch, thus recommends the indications deduced from the movements of the stars:

"The field laborer should notice the rising of the Bear, the Kids, and the luminous Dragon, with the same care the skilful pilot shows when, in order to return to his country across the stormy seas, he has to face the Hellespont or the perilous Strait of Abydos."

But to these elementary indications are added others more important, presented by observation of the signs by which "we learn to read a doubtful sky." The course of the moon and the sun, their different aspects, the form and color of the clouds, the appearance of meteors, the instinctive movement of animals, are connected with the changes of the weather, which we may foresee by an attentive study of the sky and the atmosphere. It is, moreover, evident, and Virgil well understood the fact, that this study required, in order to yield all its fruits, a series of different classes of knowledge, hardly dreamed of by antiquity: . . . "Let the Muses deign to admit me into their holy choirs! Let them teach me the track that is followed by the heavenly bodies; what cause now eclipses the light of the sun, and now the light of the moon; what secret power all at once swells the waters of the sea, pushes them beyond their limits, and then hurls them back upon themselves; why the earth shakes on its foundations; why the sun seems to hasten in winter to quench its fires in the ocean; and what obstacle, in summer, retards the approach of night."

If the inaccurate observation of natural phenomena led to erroneous or superstitious notions concerning the nature and the formation of meteors, it cannot be denied that this observation was, likewise, the basis of the knowledge that advanced the progress of meteorology, and which, spreading and growing more complete from age to age, destroyed or modified the ideas of the past, in order to substitute more rational ideas for them. "Necessary as it is," said Cicero, "to extend and confirm religion by the knowledge of Nature, it is equally so to uproot superstition."

This correct and sensible view of the case, which applies to all discoveries, to all the conquests of science, has an especial application to meteorology, whose errors, mingled with those of astrology and alchemy, have so long veiled the providential order of things that lies concealed under the apparent confusion of these phenomena.

A summing up of the errors in question, which were inseparable from the first researches that led us to the truth, might have some interest for the reader, but it would carry us too far, and we prefer to point out the actual condition of the *Meteorognosy*, " which seeks to deduce future phenomena from the observation of phenomena past and present." We borrow this definition from the excellent treatise of M. de Gasparin upon agricultural meteorology, which is about to serve us as a guide, as we shall reproduce a few passages from it, completing them, at the same time, by a concise statement of the observations most recently made.

METEOROLOGICAL PROGNOSTICATIONS FURNISHED BY THE ANIMALS.

"Animated bodies receive peculiar impressions that precede and announce change of weather. Animals appear to be endowed with an instinct in this respect, by which observers have profited, and man himself, when perfectly healthy, experiences sensations that enable him to predict, almost with certainty, the meteorological changes that are about to ensue.

"Thus, we hear distant sounds better when there is going to be rain; we also then see remote objects more distinctly, and bad odors are more offensive than usual.

"Swallows skim the ground in their flight; is it that they may feed on the worms that then come out to the surface? Lizards hide, cats make their toilet, birds oil their feathers, flies bite more sharply, chickens scratch themselves and roll in the dust, fish leap out of the water, and aquatic birds flap their wings and dabble in the ponds and brooks. Such are the results of popular observation. They have not been subjected to any severe criticism, but they have been verified often enough to be no longer subjected to doubt."

PROGNOSTICS FROM PLANTS.

"Nearly all the signs indicated announce dampness in the air, rather than the approach of rain, for they are not seen when a storm occurs in dry weather. Thus, the swelling of wood-work, which renders it difficult to close doors made of soft timber, and the contraction and tension of cordage made of vegetable fibres, are counted among the signs of atmospheric humidity. Rude hygrometers have even been constructed of these fibres. It has been noticed, also, that the flower of the pimpernel, and the stems of the trefoil and other plants, straighten themselves when the air is charged with moisture. Linnæus remarked that the African marigold opened its flowers between six and seven in the morning, and shut them at four o'clock in the afternoon, in dry weather, but that, if rain was coming, it did not open at all in the morning; that, when the Siberian thistle shuts its flower during the night, there is good weather on the next day, and that if, on the contrary, it remains open, rain may be expected."

PROGNOSTICS FROM THE STATE OF THE SKY.

"Pallor of the sun announces rain; it is seen, at such times only, through an atmosphere laden with vapors; if the heat be stifling, that too is a sign of rain, for one is then surrounded by an atmosphere saturated with vapors, and more readily heated, owing to its lack of transparency. If the vapors be collected in clouds, the sun's rays that pass through the latter heighten the temperature more than they would have done in perfectly clear weather. If the sun be clear and brilliant, it foretells a fine day; but, when the sun is at its rising preceded by redness, and this redness passes off the moment it does appear, the sign is of rain. The presumption, then, is, that the cold and vapor-laden air refracts the rays of the sun—a power that it loses as it grows heated by the rarefaction of those same vapors. The sun setting clear and cloudless in an orange-hued sky, is a sign of fine weather; if the sky be red, it is a sign of wind.

"When the sun at the horizon looks larger than usual, the sign is of rain; the same rule holds good in reference to the moon. The idea is, also, that—when the latter orb is pale, or has concentric circles more or less dark around her disk; when her horns are dull at the ends; when a luminous halo surrounds her, leading to the expression often heard among the people in France that the moon is bathing—there is going to be rain. The stars also offer similar signs; their light loses all its vividness, and they *bathe* when rain is at hand.

"The sky is bluest when there is the least vapor between it and the eye of the spectator. Upon the mountains it assumes the color of deep indigo. When the atmosphere becomes charged with vapors, it loses its transparency, and the hue of the sky becomes white, or floury, as the saying is. This sign is unequivocal. The air ceases to be transparent, also, through the effect of the winds, which agitate and carry along with them such a quantity of dust that the sky sometimes looks reddish with it, owing to the reflection of the light upon these solid corpuscles.

"The transparency of the air is not, however, always changed by the approach of rain. We have even mentioned the fact that one of the surest signs of its coming is an unusual transparent clearness, which makes distant objects seem to draw closer at such times. Thus, in one case, the lack of transparency in the air, and in the other its excess, would both be signs premonitory of rain. Facts agree with these two premises. Let us examine the circumstances:

"1. If the entire mass of air be very damp, and at a temperature sufficiently elevated to have completely dissolved the vapor; and if, at the same time, we suppose the heat to be divided between its strata so that they remain in equilibrium, there is no ascending current to diminish the transparency of the air by cooling as it ascends, and yet all the circumstances that can change the temperature—the diminution of heat as the sun declines, nocturnal radiation, and the arrival of a cold wind—lead to rain. This condition of equilibrium in the strata, joined to their almost complete saturation with vapor, is noticed particularly in summer, and it is then that distant objects seem near at hand.

"2. It also happens that the higher range of clouds will sometimes form a sort of dome above our heads, and then, since we are in comparative obscurity, the objects that are lighted up seem nearer to us. We recall with pleasure the superb spectacle that such an arrangement of the sky presented to us on the summit of Mont Ventoux.

The entire horizon was clear, but the mountain was capped with a heavy mass of black clouds, which threw us into gloom. We were then enabled to witness something that we never could see again in other ascensions that we made—the entire sweep of the eastern Pyrenees and the coasts of the Mediterranean to where they turn southward to regain Catalonia. A moment afterward, a cloud overspread the sky and a heavy rain fell over that whole region, the atmosphere of which was, no doubt, in the state of equilibrium that we have described above.

"The winds also are indications of the weather to ensue, not only through their own qualities, but also by means of the study of the higher winds, whose presence and direction are known by the movement of the clouds. When the lower wind strengthens greatly, and the clouds move in contrary directions, on lines that make a quite open angle, the inference is, that the lower wind is about to yield its place to the upper one.

"Two winds of opposite qualities, succeeding each other, often bring rain. Thus, a cold wind, entering an atmosphere impregnated with moisture by the warm wind that preceded it, will bring about a precipitation of water; and the same will be the case where a damp, warm wind enters air that had been chilled by the wind that had preceded it.

"Generally, an approaching rain can be better foreseen when the sky presents several banks, or layers of clouds, resting one above the other. The winds that carry with them detached masses of clouds yield but light rains.

"Motionless clouds, lying in the quarter whence the wind blows, bring only a continuance of that wind; but, if they appear in the opposite quarter, they announce its termination.

"Clouds coming up simultaneously, yet impelled by different winds, announce an early storm.

"Clouds accumulating on the sides of mountains foretell rain.

"Mists that disperse completely, without forming clouds, accompany fine weather, because they prove that the air retains the faculty of dissolving vapor; but many days of mist in succession lead almost with certainty to rain."

Let us add to these signs a few collected by Admiral Fitzroy, and quoted in his "Instructions on the Use of the Barometer."

"The following are the signs most familiar to navigators and farmers:

"A rosy sky at sunset, fine weather. A red

sky in the morning, bad weather or a great deal of wind.

"A gray sky in the morning, fine weather. If the first light of dawn appear over a bed of clouds, wind may be looked for. If on the horizon, fine weather.

"Light clouds with imperfectly-defined edges announce fine weather and moderate breezes. Thick clouds with well-marked edges, wind. A deep, dark-blue sky of sombre tinge indicates wind. A clear and brilliant-blue sky indicates fine weather. The lighter the clouds look, the less reason is there to anticipate wind. The more dense, the more rolled together, twisted, and tattered, they are, the stronger the wind will be. A brilliant-yellow sky at sunset announces wind; a pale-yellow one, rain. According to the predominance of red, yellow, or grayish tints, we can foretell the condition of the weather with a very close approximation to accuracy.

"Small clouds of an inky color portend rain. Light clouds, moving rapidly in the direction opposite to dense masses, announce wind and rain.

"High clouds passing before the sun, the moon, or the stars, in a direction opposite to that pursued by the lower beds of clouds, or of the wind felt at the surface of the soil, indicate a change of wind.

"After fine weather, the first signs of a change are ordinarily high white clouds, in belts or in light dappled tufts, or locks, which grow larger, and soon form dense and sombre masses. Generally, the more remote and higher up these clouds appear, the less abrupt the change of weather will be, but it will be considerable.

"Soft, light, delicate tints, with clouds of decided shape, indicate or accompany fine weather. Extraordinary tints and dense clouds, with hard outlines, indicate rain and probably a gale of wind.

"Remark the clouds that form on hills and other elevated places, and cling there. If they continue there, augment, or descend, they indicate rain. If they, however, ascend and disperse, they portend good weather. When sea-birds fly out away from land in the morning, there will be fine weather and moderate winds. If they remain near the shore, or fly inland, gales and storms may be expected. Many other animals are susceptible to atmospheric changes, and these indications should not be neglected.

"Thus, when birds that usually fly in flocks, swallows for instance, keep near to their nests, flying from one side to the other and skimming the ground, the sign is of rain or wind. When domestic animals seek sheltered places, when chimneys smoke, or when, in calm weather, the smoke does not ascend overhead, bad weather may be expected.

"When the sky is remarkably clear at the horizon, and objects usually invisible are distinguishable from each other, or appear higher up by refraction, there will be rain and perhaps wind.

"Extraordinary brilliance of the stars, lack of distinctness, or apparent multiplication of the horns of the moon, halos, and fragments of rainbows upon detached clouds, indicate that the wind will increase, and that there will be rain."

M. Marié-Davy, in his "Instructions on the Use of the Barometer," for foretelling changes of the weather, has given the result of a comparative examination of the meteorological charts of the Observatory, and, in so doing, has summed up all that is known at the present day concerning the movements of the atmosphere on the surface of Europe. These instructions contain very interesting details relative to the advance and movement of the whirlwinds that take place in the great aërial current, the general direction of which exerts a preponderating influence over the meteorological condition of the European countries.

Other observations were recommended by the

International Conference held at Brussels in 1853, on the invitation of the United States, with a view to adopt a common system of meteorological observations at sea. Thus, thunder-storms and tornadoes that occur in the vicinity of the great oceanic currents; the drift of floating ice; the appearance of land birds and insects out at sea; showers of dust; red or white spots that are frequently remarked on the surface of the deep; the number and direction of the shooting-stars; the northern lights, and similar phenomena, might give some very useful indications concerning the course and formation of the meteoric phenomena, which cannot be foreseen with any fixed degree of accuracy, excepting by first taking the utmost care to collate and arrange observations of every kind relative to the circumstances in which they occur.

CHARACTER OF FUTURE SEASONS AND YEARS.

The attempt has been made to foretell the character of seasons and years to come, but the insufficiency of the data on which the prognostics were based has, thus far, rendered the endeavor nearly fruitless.

Nevertheless, M. de Gasparin reports that, in 1829, M. Hubert-Burnaud, of Yverdon, predicted a severe winter for 1830, and it came as he had said. "This was no prophecy," M. Burnaud tells us, " but a very simple calculation. South and southwest winds having prevailed for six months, I had a right to suppose that the north winds would have their turn. In the second place, the sun having been hidden during the months of July and October, it was natural to think that the earth would be cooled, at its surface, more than usual. This circumstance, combined with the presence of the north wind, should render the winter a very cold one. Finally, the autumn having been very rainy, the winter, according to all appearances, would be dry. When all these circumstances are partial only, no conclusion can be drawn; but their general prevalence, throughout Europe, would be likely to produce simple effects, because there would be no disturbing cause over an immense extent of space."

Let us add that, in his important memoir on the periodicity of severe winters, published in the *Annuaire de la Société Météorologique de France*, in May, 1861, M. Renou, a learned meteorologist, has grouped together all the observations recorded since the year 1400, and has deduced from them some remarkable results in reference to the periodical return of severe winters.

"There will soon be an opportunity," says M. Renou, "to verify the fact whether the periodicity that I have announced for rigorous winters does really exist, since the hardest winter of all is to occur about 1861, and cannot, in my opinion, experience a delay of more than two years, as was the case in 1709. Any postponement, I also believe, would be compensated by an exceptional intensity of the season."

The winter of 1860 and that of 1863 and '64, which covered southern Europe with snow and ice, and was very severe even in Egypt, partially confirmed M. Renou's predictions. We may be permitted, then, to hope that the possibility of foretelling the meteorological character of certain years or certain periods, when based upon more numerous and accurate observations, may one day be sufficiently ascertained to lead to important results, particularly in reference to agriculture, the leading source of our wealth and comfort.

SHOOTING-STARS.—INFLUENCE OF THE MOON.

We must here mention the researches of M. Coulvier-Gravier, in relation to the shooting-stars, whose appearance and direction enable us to foretell changes of weather two or three days in advance. The facts collated by this indefatigable observer in his work entitled "Researches in relation to Meteors and the Laws that govern Them," published at Paris in 1863, are sufficiently remarkable to merit a serious examination, and it is to be desired that the interesting researches which he has taken up should be multiplied in number, so as to ascertain their practical utility. Moreover, we have already indicated all the importance of these researches, which will aid us in attaining a better comprehension of the limits and constitution of the atmosphere, the first foundation of a more exact knowledge of meteors, and the laws that govern their formation.

The influence of the moon upon atmospheric phenomena, the weather, and the seasons, admitted as it has been, by mariners, since the days of antiquity, and occupying so large a place as it does in the ancient collections of agricultural maxims, was long denied by most men of learning, or regarded by them as too weak to produce any appreciable results. It is, nevertheless, beyond all doubt that the attraction of the moon and the sun, which produces the tides of the ocean, occasions atmospheric tides, also; and it is very probable, indeed, that the latter may, especially at epochs when they are the strongest, determine changes in the condition of the weather.

Experiments made with the utmost care, by the aid of the barometer, have indicated the totality of the movement imparted to the atmosphere by the phases of the moon, and the general influence of those phases on the rains and on the direction of the wind is now recognized. But it is not easy to separate it for each place from the secondary causes that tend to disguise it, and it can be reached only by multiplying observations, at present so very incomplete, with a view to establish the probability of periodical variations of the weather corresponding with the different phases of the moon.

M. Arago, in a remarkable dissertation * relative to the influence of the lunar phases on atmospheric phenomena and the vegetable realm, has established incontestable facts which, while destroying errors hitherto accepted, still prove that popular notions on the subject are not altogether without foundation. When based upon real observation, they, on the contrary, may render good service, unless they should become more injurious than useful through the too great importance attached to them. M. de Gasparin says, very justly

---

* "Annuaire of the Bureau of Longitude. 1832, 1833." See also, in the "Annales Hydrographiques," 1st trimestre of 1864, the note on Meteorology by Admiral Fitzroy

on this subject, that "there are scientific prejudices, as there are popular prejudices, but in no age have learned men been more disposed to give up theirs, and to submit them, in good faith, to the crucible of experiment and observation. The people themselves, too, no longer cling with the same tenacity to their superstitious ideas, and manifest much greater readiness to listen to the voice of reason."

CHAPTER XII.

PRACTICAL METEOROLOGY.

The Brussels Conference.—Meteorological Practice.—Instruments of Observation.—Telegraphic Meteorology.—The Hurricane of December 2, 1863.—Alarm-Signals.—Rural Meteorology.—Association for the Advancement of Meteorology.

THE BRUSSELS CONFERENCE.

ADMIRAL FITZROY has collected, in an excellent work called "The Book of the Weather," published at London in 1863, the most familiar notions concerning meteorology, and has made known the combinations recently adopted in the principal observatories of Europe and the United States, in order to be able to give, either daily or on the approach of storms, some rational announcement of the anticipated change in the weather. We have summed up, in a work entitled "Storms," with very considerable fulness of detail, the substance of what has been done, up to the present time, to attain this important result; and we have shown, by enumerating the services already rendered, all that could be hoped for in the early future. Returning here, briefly, to the same subject, we are happy that we have it in our power to bear testimony to the rapid progress realized since the organization of the Imperial Observatory at Paris, a progress that leaves no doubt remaining as to the rank that meteorology is destined to take among the most useful of the sciences, and those that are best adapted to aid man in his labors, by giving him a more correct idea of the universal order that presides over all things.

It is to a learned officer, formerly of the United States naval service, Commander Maury, that we owe the first idea of a great association to unite all the most advanced nations in one common system of meteorological observations, and intended to include the entire globe, or at least all those regions to which the light of science and civilization has penetrated in our day.

A conference, in which the principal states of Europe were represented, met at Brussels in 1853, M. Quételet, the director of the Royal Observatory at Brussels, presiding. The object was, as we have said, to come to an understanding in reference to the adoption of a uniform system of observations at sea. Maury, who was then the director of the National Observatory at Washington, represented his government at this meeting, and we here quote a part of his address, in which he explained to those present the purpose of his mission:

"The proposition, in consequence of which the American Government has thought fit to call for the present meeting, emanates from the English Government. It consists of the communication of a project drawn up by Captain Henry James of the Royal Engineers, by order of Sir John Burgoyne, inspector-general of fortifications, and in which the Government of the United States was invited to take part.

"Nineteen stations have been established by England, in pursuance of a uniform system, and the observations have been placed under the immediate direction of the officer of engineers commanding at each station.

"The American Government accepted the proposal of the English Government, and, on condition that the plan of observation should be extended to the sea and made universal, promised its coöperation. I was then intrusted with the duty of placing myself in communication with the owners and the captains of the naval and mercantile marine, for the execution of the plan.

"It was by the aid of information extracted from more than a thousand log-books that I have been enabled to prepare the charts of tracks, winds, and currents, that have been published up to the present time.

"In order to give still more extension to nautical observations, the Government of the United States has decided that an appeal should be made to all maritime nations to induce them to adopt a uniform model of log-book.

"The aim of our assembling is, therefore, to come to a common understanding with reference to a uniform method of nautical and meteorological observations taken at sea. I am already indebted to the courtesy of one of the members present, M. Jansen, lieutenant in the navy of the Netherlands, for an extract from the log-book kept on board of a Dutch man-of-war, and it may be cited as an example of what may be expected of expert and careful observers. In order to secure regularity in the distribution of the charts that the American Government offers gratuitously to captains of every nationality, I would express the wish that a person should be designated by the government of each country to collect and compile the extracts from log-books to which I have had the honor of calling your attention. It is through his hands that the charts would be conveyed to the parties for whom they were destined."

We shall not here enumerate all the resolutions adopted by the Conference, as we did in a work entitled "The Phenomena of the Sea and the Atmosphere," and more special in its nature. But we think it right to recall the fact that it was the starting-point for the researches which have extended so far since then, and have been the source of important progress in meteorology. May we not be allowed, at the same time, to remark that, if the most wonderful of the Divine works, in the order of material things, be the power of the laws that maintain the harmony of the universe, there is in the moral order no more gratifying subject of contemplation than the laws which govern the progress of communities, and which stand forth in better relief in our day, in the happy tendencies of Christianity toward association—in other words, toward union of sentiment and effort?

The Meteorological Bureau of Utrecht, under the direction of M. Buys Ballot, a learned professor, and established in order to centralize the observations made by the navy of Holland, was the first establishment in Europe that coöperated with Commander Maury's labors. Lieutenant Jansen, a distinguished officer, who from the outset had applied himself with the most intelligent zeal to the new system of research pursued on the ocean, was attached to this bureau.

Belgium, Sweden, Norway, Denmark, Portugal, Spain, the free city of Hamburg, and the republic of Bremen, soon followed the example set by Holland. The British Government also was one of the first to establish a bureau commissioned to arrange and discuss the observations collected by English ships upon all the waters of the globe, in accordance with the plan recommended by the Brussels Conference. Most of the great Powers, also, had accepted this plan, and expressed their intention to put it in execution, by means of the vessels sailing under their flag. These, to use Commander Maury's expression, would, for the time being, have been made so many floating observatories, on board of which our common effort for the advancement of science and the good of humanity would be going on.

METEOROLOGICAL PRACTICE.

But it was easy to foresee that the ocean could not remain the only subject of systematic study, and Maury subsequently asked for another conference, with a view to proposing a plan of terrestrial observations, "so that meteorology should be enabled, at last, to move onward in a path truly universal."

It is evident that in this direction alone can we hope to discover the great laws that govern the movements of the atmosphere—laws of which we now have but a glimpse, and the knowledge of which would furnish the most solid foundation to meteorological studies.

The nature of the researches necessary to attain this result, not only demands the widest range of observation, but those engaged in it must be able to correspond with such rapidity as to announce the appearance of phenomena, and to follow their progress; and the employment of the electric telegraph has arisen to give meteorology this powerful means of investigation.

It is around the great lakes of America, where disasters are so frequent, that this system of communication was first put in play to signal the approach of storms; adopted, subsequently, by the principal states of Europe, it has already rendered the greatest service to navigators, and should likewise aid in diminishing the losses that unexpected bad weather so often inflicts upon agriculture.

INSTRUMENTS OF OBSERVATION. 293

Rapidly organized in England, thanks to the zeal and devotion of Admiral Fitzroy, the system of telegraphic warnings has been inaugurated in France also, through the efforts of an illustrious *savant*, M. le Verrier, the director of the Imperial Observatory. The ministry of marine in that country has, also, on its part, decreed the establishment of a meteorological service in the seaports, combined with the similar service in England, and the recent construction, along the whole extent of the French sea-coast, of signal-light houses connected with the grand net-work of electric telegraphs, admits of the transmission of warnings to all the threatened points, and even to vessels that may be passing in sight of the coast. It may be readily understood how the generalization of such a surface is as advantageous to the interests of navigation as to the progress of science, and we shall see this still more clearly as we take up some details of the organization of meteorological observatories.

INSTRUMENTS OF OBSERVATION.

Among the instruments of physical science which serve to determine atmospheric variations, the barometer is one of those that are most usually consulted. All mariners have had the opportunity to remark the usefulness of the indications that it yields previously to rain and gales of wind. But these indications, being relative to the weight of the column of air that causes the column of mercury to oscillate, do not tell us in what case that weight increases or diminishes, and, in order to arrive at a more exact foreknowledge of phenomena, it is necessary to ascertain, by the thermometer and the hygrometer, the different causes that may influence the weight of the atmospheric strata. Thus, for example, the variation of these two instruments, especially during the winter season, may indicate, in the absence of barometrical signs, the approach of cold and dry north winds, or warm and moist south winds, the predominance of which determines the character of the weather.

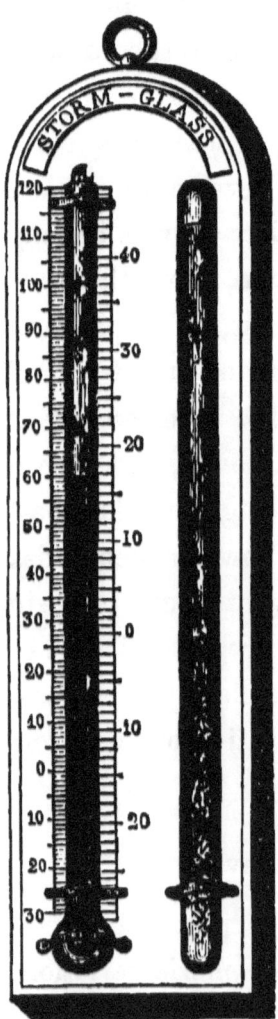

If these winds, in their general character, differ,

as Admiral Fitzroy thinks they do, and as we should feel inclined to admit, in their electrical condition, the indications of a curious instrument entitled the storm-glass must not be neglected, that condition no doubt having a great influence upon the atmospheric phenomena, that may modify the pressure of the atmosphere.

The storm-glass, used in England more than a century ago, and taken up again by Admiral Fitzroy, is composed of a glass tube, hermetically sealed, containing a chemical mixture, the aspect of which varies according to the direction of the wind, and not according to its force; that is to say, remarks the admiral, "according to the special character, and very probably according to the electric tension, of the aërial current."

We have had the opportunity to watch the workings of one of these instruments for several months, and we have often seen it indicate with remarkable precision the violent storms of the north, and the abundant rains that accompany the great aërial currents of the south.

Still other instruments are employed in the observatories, as, for instance, the psychrometer, or damp-bulb thermometer, which indicates the quantity of vapor in the atmosphere; the pluviometer, which marks the quantity of rain fallen;

the surface plate, by which the force of the wind is measured through the pressure exerted upon it; the electrometer, that notes the electricity in the air; the prepared papers, by the exposure of which to the atmosphere, and their subsequent comparison with each other, the quantity of ozone or electrified oxygen is ascertained through its property of modifying their colors; and, finally, certain special instruments destined to indicate the magnetic condition of the earth.

TELEGRAPHIC METEOROLOGY.

It is evident that the atmospheric condition of any region is subjected to the influence of the surrounding, and, in certain circumstances, to that of other very distant, regions. An observatory daily receiving, from all the chief points of a wide extent of territory, like that which embraces Europe and the banks of the Mediterranean, telegrams stating the condition of the weather at each of those points, could not only preannounce the atmospheric variations for the place in which it is situated, but likewise for each of the places with which it is in correspondence. Such is now the position of the most important observatories of Europe, and principally of the one in Paris, which has been justly designated by Admiral Fitzroy as "a grand centre of telegraphic alliance."

This observatory now publishes daily a bulletin containing the data that are collected there every three hours, as well as those that are furnished to it at eight o'clock in the morning, by about fifty correspondents distributed over the whole surface of Europe. These data embrace the barometric pressure, the temperature, the direction and the force of the lower strata of winds, the state of the sky, and the condition of the sea upon the coast, at each station. Along with the meteorological chart of the day, prepared under the direction of M. Marie-Davy, is a summary statement of the general character of the atmosphere, drawn up by that distinguished *savant*, with a forecast of the probable state of the weather on the ensuing day. These probabilities have reference to fourteen regions, or districts, into which the European seaboard has been marked off.

Curves corresponding to the barometric pressure, divided by intervals of five millimetres, are traced on this meteorological chart. The pressure of the atmosphere in Europe experiences frequent variations, and it is in the proximity or separation of those curves that the principal elements of a rational foreknowledge of the weather are to be found.

THE HURRICANE OF DECEMBER 2.

This useful application of telegraphic meteorology was scarcely realized when a terrible hurricane occurred to demonstrate its efficacy. This hurricane, which was analogous to the cyclones of the tropical regions, swept across France between the 2d and the 4th of December, 1863. Its influence was felt as early as the 28th of November, the time when it was on the ocean, as high up in latitude as the south of Spain. On the 27th and the 28th the bulletin had already announced the condition of the atmosphere as very doubtful. Until the 1st of December, the whirlwind ascended toward the north, and was then signalled from the northwest of England. "The rapid fall which has been noted this morning in Ireland," said M. Marie-Davy, "the position of the curves of equal barometric pressure, and the easterly trending of the winds, which have gathered strength in the south and southwest, show that this phenomenon is inclining eastwardly, to strike the coasts of Europe toward the north of England. The storm, which will probably extend over all France, seems likely to be severe." And, in fact, on the morning of the 2d, the mercury fell with extreme rapidity in England and France. The whirlwind had then swept down upon the former country, and had its centre near Liverpool.

As early as the 30th, the seaports from Dunkirk to Nantes had been forewarned by telegraph that they were threatened with a gale. On the 1st of December, at noon, all the ocean-ports were notified that a heavy storm, coming from the southwest, was bearing down upon England and France. Dispatches sent on the 2d will give some idea of the activity that the meteorological service displays in perilous circumstances:

"At eight o'clock in the morning, the storm did, in fact, burst upon the north and a part of the west of France. Paris and Bordeaux feel a violent wind, but at Lyons, Limoges, and Bayonne, the wind is still weak.

"At noon, all the ports of the Mediterranean were again informed that they were seriously threatened. Madrid received the same dispatch in reference to the seaports on the Gulf of Lyons. Turin was likewise notified for the north coasts of Italy and as far as Leghorn. At fifty minutes past one, it was repeated for the benefit of the ports along the coasts from Civita Vecchia to Palermo."

Admiral Fitzroy's telegrams had also notified our ocean-ports in advance. They announced that the English coasts were covered with the warning signals.

The Observatory of Paris remained for some time without knowing whether its last dispatches had reached their destination. Along several lines the storm had prostrated the telegraph-poles and broken the wires. But communication remained open for a length of time sufficient for the transmission of the most important telegram: " On the 2d of December, during the daytime, I received the two dispatches stating that a severe storm was about to traverse France," writes the president of the Toulon Chamber of Commerce to M. le Verrier. " They were published and posted up immediately, and the merchant-vessels in the roadstead had time to provide, and did so provide, against all risks. The maritime prefecture, on its behalf, directed all officers who were ashore to hasten on board of their vessels. The storm burst forth with all its fury about half-past three o'clock in the afternoon. The first telegram sent on the 2d, confirming that of the day before, had therefore gained four hours' time ahead of the storm, and every thing was ready to meet the emergency. Thanks to the precautions thus taken, there was no damage, no disaster to deplore."

The telegrams forwarded to Turin were immediately communicated to the ports on the western coast of Italy. The following note was published on the 3d in the *Giornale di Genova* (Genoese Journal):

"The prediction of the Paris Observatory was fully realized. The first signs of the storm were felt yesterday about 7.30 P. M. During the night it raged furiously; but there appears, nevertheless, to have been no disastrous occurrence in our neighborhood. The commandant of the port had hastened to take all proper measures, and we may be thankful for them."

As soon as the principal ports of the Channel and the Ocean had received the warning telegrams, they communicated them to the entire coast by means of the electric signal stations that have recently been established there. The number of disasters was, however, great enough in those waters to cause surprise. Relatively to the direction of the wind, which beat on the coast as a general thing, it was more difficult to take precautions, and, on the other hand, again, there must have been some negligence in regard to them.

The best ideas penetrate the minds of men but slowly, and there are, unfortunately, many navigators still who do not take the warnings thus telegraphed to them seriously enough. For a considerable period it required special instructors in England to give sailors and fishermen more accurate ideas on this subject.

The storm burst upon the northern coasts of France with extreme suddenness and violence. At Cherbourg, for instance, there was very little wind and sea in the morning; small boats could navigate in the offing. The barometer, however, coincided with the warnings given, in marking signs of bad weather. At eight o'clock it had gone down seven hundred and thirty-seven millimetres. At ten o'clock the storm came on like a clap of thunder. Parts of buildings were knocked down, and roofs torn off. In the roadstead, the sea was hurled aloft in whirling masses, and formed a thick curtain of sprayey mist. Enormous billows beat over the breakwater.

A pinnace, belonging to the iron-clad frigate *La Couronne*, had set out to assist a merchant vessel that was nearly in a sinking condition. After reaching it, the pinnace was towing it in to moorings when the storm burst forth with its full fury. A small steamer from the port came to its assistance for some time, but was obliged to drop the tow in order to escape sinking itself. The tide was running out, and, while the vessel was borne onward to be wrecked on a less perilous beach, the pinnace was carried out to sea. It was lost to view, and in the evening two sailors, covered with cuts and bruises, and both insensible, were picked up near Cape Levi. They had but a confused recollection of the disaster, and were the sole survivors of the boat's crew, which was commanded by M. de Besplas, a gallant officer. The men were intrepid, and, led by a worthy chief, did not hesitate to sacrifice their life in order to accomplish an act of self-devotion and humanity.

The reports from London declared that no such formidable storm had been seen there since 1823. It everywhere presented the same character as at Cherbourg, excepting differences in the direction of the wind and in the secondary phenomena. At Strasburg, it was not until the 3d, about four o'clock in the afternoon, that heavy clouds covered the sky in a moment. Immediately, rain, snow, and hail, driven by a furious wind, drenched the streets and squares. In the south, on the contrary, a dry and cold north wind blew a storm, at first under a clear sky.

The Observatory proposed to make a study of this storm, as a totality, by means of the exact indications procurable at all the stations lying within its range. This study, the first part of which was published in the *Bulletin* of March 31, 1864, will, no doubt, be very prolific of results for meteorological science, as were the similar labors of Admiral Fitzroy, after the great storm of October, 1859.

The theory of cyclones, founded by the Redfields, the Reids, and the Piddingtons, embraces the general laws of their translation and rotation. It has furnished practical rules for the management of vessels; but it still leaves many gaps, which the new studies of to-day, aided by the electric telegraph, will powerfully assist in filling.— The point of view taken by the Observatory appears to us, moreover, excellent, and we earnestly hope that the extension of the meteorological service will soon render it possible to extend these researches over a larger basis.*

"If our charts," said M. Marie-Davy, in a note sent in to the Academy of Sciences, " enable us to foretell a storm, and to follow it in its course across the Continent of Europe, they tell us nothing, or almost nothing, concerning the place of their origin and their mode of formation, and nevertheless that is one of the essential elements, not

---

* In M. Marie-Davy's interesting work entitled "The Movements of the Atmosphere and the Sea, considered in reference to Foretelling the State of the Weather."

only of the science, but of its application. We attach the greatest importance to the construction of daily charts, embracing the whole Northern Hemisphere, were it to require a whole year to bring together the necessary elements for each one of them. In the midst of the incessant shifting and changing of atmospheric phenomena, the important point is, very certainly, to extract from them great general laws, and the search for these may be aided by the investigations of preceding years."

ALARM-SIGNALS.

The alarm-signals employed in England to announce the approach of storms consist, in the daytime, of three figures made of strong canvas, which are hoisted on the mast of the signal-stations, and can be seen at a great distance.

A cone, with the point turned toward the sky, announces that there is some likelihood of a storm from the north.

Placed with its point downward, the cone indicates the approach of a storm from the south.

A cylinder is the signal for a hurricane or a rotating tempest.

If the cone be placed with the point upward above the cylinder, the storm that threatens comes from the north.

If the cone, on the contrary, be under the cylinder, with its point turned toward the ground, the hurricane comes from the south.

During the night, lanterns, arranged as they are seen in the accompanying illustration, in such manner as to represent the cones or the cylinder, take the place of the day-signals.

These signals, which are very simple, and of easy manipulation, will, no doubt, be generally adopted wherever the organization of the meteorological service is such as to admit of the preannouncement of storms.

On the coasts of the kingdom of Italy, mariners are forewarned that a storm threatens them by a red flag hoisted on all the towers and lighthouses of the principal localities, ranging from Genoa to Palermo, and thence up along the Adriatic.

This signal is employed only when it may be inferred from the meteorological *Bulletin*, sent by the director of the Observatory at Paris, that a tempest is approaching. The telegram that announces it is moreover posted up in all the seaports, and transmitted to the Chambers of Commerce.

On the most dangerous points of the coast of England, where the fishing-boats and small craft,

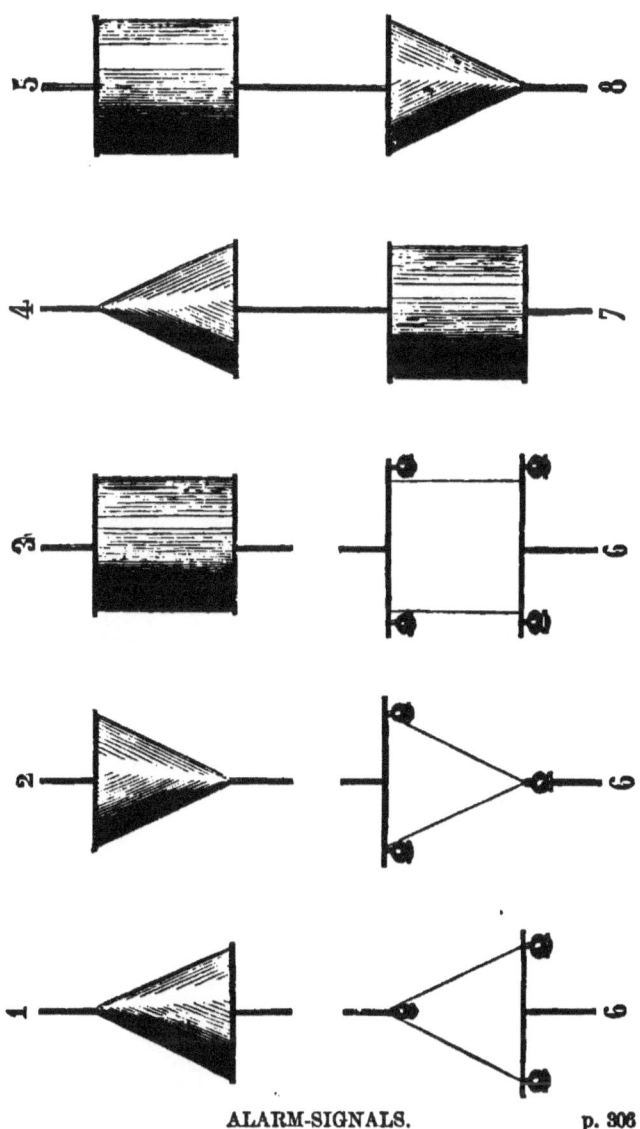

ALARM-SIGNALS. p. 306

that perform the service of the coast, are exposed to formidable gales, even during the fine season, barometers put up by the meteorological bureau assist in foretelling bad weather. French ocean-ports have received from the ministry of the marine instruments destined for the same service; and the recent adoption by France and England of a code of signals that offers to all nations a uniform means of communicating at sea, will enable vessels provided with the necessary material, the price of which is very moderate, to put themselves in communication with the signal-stations, and to receive the latest meteorological warnings from them.

AGRICULTURAL METEOROLOGY.

M. le Verrier—in his reply to the ministry of Public Instruction, on the subject of the observations that it would be possible to organize in France, in order to obtain data useful to agriculture—recently said: "The reception, accorded by our maritime populations, of the warnings furnished them by the Observatory causes us to foresee the time at hand when our farmers will claim similar attention from the solicitude of the government.

"Your excellency will, no doubt, remember

that it was the urgent request of Prussia, on behalf of a society of agriculturists at Mecklenburg, that gave occasion to our first dispatches predicting the state of the weather, and that as early as 1854, after a storm that had devastated Provence, after having raged at Havre twenty-four hours earlier, the Agricultural Board of Toulon (Var) addressed a long letter to the Minister of Agriculture, in order to set forth to him the advantages that would result from the preannouncement, at the right time, of the approach of bad weather.

"I think, then, M. Minister, that not only is there fair occasion to encourage the good intentions of the Normal School of Vesoul, which asked for authority to have its pupils, under the direction of a master, daily take meteorological observations, to be published in the *Journal of Practical Agriculture*, but that there would be great utility in extending this measure to all the normal schools in the empire. No one would hesitate for a moment to take charge of this work.

"The instruments necessary for each school are:

A barometer	80 francs
A thermometer	20 "
A pluviometer	30 "
An hygrometer	25 "
Total	155 francs.

AGRICULTURAL METEOROLOGY. 309

"The agricultural societies, the rural boards, and the councils-general, could contribute the means to defray this expense.

"Meteorology is taking a rank less and less disputed among our sciences of general application, and public attention is fixed upon the services it is called upon to render to our people. The moment seems, then, to have arrived for serious effort in organizing the means of study that are indispensable to it."

In a subsequent letter M. le Verrier called the attention of the Minister of Public Instruction to the numerous tempests that crossed over Europe during the month of May, 1864, and, in remarking the fact that the storm-gusts of summer seem to "have the same origin as the great tempests of the bad season, and that both may be followed, as well as foreseen, in their progress by the same means," he asked the concurrence of the normal schools, the Chambers of Commerce, the agricultural societies, and government engineers, in getting together the materials of a good statistical statement of storms, that would render it possible to prepare charts of the regions traversed by those meteors, and determine the probabilities of storms for each district. It will be easily understood that such charts might not merely assist in forewarning farmers, but that they would, moreover, present a means of proportioning the sacrifices each individual would have to make, in a system of mutual insurance, to his chances of loss.

In reply to this letter, the minister saw fit to issue a circular to the prefects, asking the concurrence of the council-general of each department in providing the necessary instruments, so as to put the normal schools in a position to collect the observations indicated by M. le Verrier.

If we consider, as Messrs. Payen and Barral have done, in their remarkable report * upon the possible application of meteorology to agriculture, all the advantages that would result to our rural districts from a knowledge of the weather based upon observations more certain than the usual signs, we may hope that one day each of our villages, like each of our seaports, will possess the necessary meteorological instruments, obtained either by means of a moderate assessment or a contribution from the townships and communes. The tutor might be intrusted with the daily observations, which are easy to record; and the instructions adopted † by the committee of the scien-

* Bulletin of the Imperial Observatory, number of July 19, 1864.
† Bulletin of the Imperial Observatory, number of August 25, 1864, and following numbers.

tific association, of which we shall mention the organization farther on, would soon enable him to foresee and preannounce, in most cases, the approach of atmospheric disturbances. Intelligent property-owners, in associating themselves also with these investigations, would not only obtain indications calculated to aid rural pursuits : "They will always be certain," says M. de Gasparin, "of finding a pleasant and useful occupation in meteorological observations; in their comparison with those of other places and other times, and, while amusing their leisure hours, they will be paving the way to the period when meteorology will acquire the certainty of deduction which it now lacks, and when conjectures relative to future phenomena will become probabilities."

Let us add that the comparison of series of observations made at different periods may indicate, according to the just remark of M. Buys-Ballot, whether the natural condition of the place has undergone changes, in consequence of the cultivation of the ground, or the clearing away of forests, the drying up of lakes, arms of the sea, or marshes, or by the replanting of woods. These indications could not, undoubtedly, acquire a scientific value, excepting by the lapse of time, but they would be infinitely precious to us, should they go to confirm the influence that man may exercise over the character of climate by a wise management of the domain confided to him.

ASSOCIATION FOR THE ADVANCEMENT OF METEOROLOGY.

The Meteorological Society of France, in publishing since 1849 a yearly *Annuaire*, or Calendar, intended to comprise all the experiments and observations which had been but little known until that time, and, to stimulate fresh researches, has powerfully contributed to the progress of the studies relating to a knowledge of the atmosphere and of the phenomena taking place in it. Under the auspices of this society, M. Renou, one of its members, has recently commenced a course of meteorology in the grand amphitheatre of the School of Medicine. This course, in showing the importance of the new science, accessible as it is to all ranges of intellect, will give a new impulse to the useful research and to the interesting observations that it invites one to pursue.

The zealous director of the *Journal of Practical Agriculture*, M. Barral, has brought about the formation of a meteorological net-work based upon the free coöperation of the farmers, and it, in permitting the monthly publication of notes

ADVANCEMENT OF METEOROLOGY. 313

on the condition of the crops, at the same time furnishes the best documents we have on the climatology of France.

Finally, an important society for the advancement of astronomy and meteorology has recently been established under the presidency of M. le Verrier. The following extract from the minutes of the first general sitting, which took place on the 3d of June, 1864, will make known its object:

"Astronomy and meteorology are making rapid progress in the Old as well as in the New World, thanks to the coöperation of governments, individual action, and powerful associations; numerous establishments have been founded, and great works accomplished, under this triple impulsion.

"The French Government stands in the first rank of those that give a liberal and fruitful support to science. The cities of Toulouse, and Marseilles are erecting observatories, on their own behalf, and the Chamber of Commerce of Toulon has founded a yearly prize for meteorological observations at sea.

"The Association for the Advancement of Astronomy and Meteorology has for its object the completion of the means of action at the disposal of France." *

After this exposition, presented to the meeting by M. le Verrier, the committee intrusted with the first propositions relative to meteorology, represented by M. Renou, made a report, of which we reproduce the principal passages:

"Meteorology is one of the sciences that were cultivated in the earliest times. The diversity of climates on the surface of the globe; the changes that daily take place in the state of the heavens; in the degree of movement, heat, and dampness of the atmosphere; and, above all, those great commotions of the air that disturb the surface of the earth and the sea, concern our safety and comfort too nearly not to have been interesting to mankind at all times.

"It belonged, however, to our day, in which Science advances at so rapid a pace, and has at her disposal so many resources hitherto unknown, to give meteorology a prolific impulse by extending her investigations over the whole surface of the globe, and associating individual efforts by the rapid intercommunication of results obtained.

---

* This association counts more than two thousand members, among whom are a great many ladies. An assessment of ten francs per annum is levied.

"The services rendered to navigation by Maury, and by those who have striven to walk in his footsteps, show that meteorology has entered its true path. There can no longer be any doubt that, by combined researches carried on perseveringly, upon a scale growing continually broader and more comprehensive, it must attain a knowledge of laws, as yet unknown, that govern the motions of the atmosphere, and thus at last give us the key of what we call the caprices of the weather.

"The committee was struck with the importance of the position already given to meteorology by the initiative of France, by the efforts of all the nations of Europe, and by the eager coöperation of all the managing boards of the telegraphic lines of France and different countries."

After having made known the great international meteorological service of which the Imperial Observatory of Paris is, at present, the centre, M. Renou adds:

"An association of this kind is incontestably a fact of great value, and the end at which it aims is most important, since it embraces the prevention of those disasters that annually cost the lives of thousands of men, and the loss of millions of property."

M. Renou then took up the question of establishing prizes, for meteorological investigations, to be founded by the society. These prizes, three in number, are to be bestowed upon the authors of the best treatises on the general movements of the atmosphere; the best observations at sea; and the best series of observations made at places but little known. Since then, two new prizes have been instituted, to be given to the authors of the two best treatises relative to the application of meteorology to agricultural questions.

A chart summing up the service of nautical meteorology, the centre of which is at Paris, has been distributed to the members of the association. This service, by which warnings of bad weather are communicated, now extends to all the coasts of the Baltic Sea, to that of the North Sea, to the French coasts of the Channel and the Ocean, to the coasts of Portugal and Spain, to the French coasts of the Mediterranean, to those of Italy, of Sicily, of the Adriatic, as far as Albania, and, finally, to the Russian coasts of the Black Sea.

At the first session above noted, the association voted an appropriation applicable to the construction of a large telescope, to be put up in one of the large cities of Southern France.

The links that unite astronomy, meteorology,

and the physical constitution of the globe, were treated with great elevation of views by Father Secchi, the director of the observatory at Rome, in a series of memoranda relative to the connection observed between the variations of the atmosphere and those of the magnetism of the earth. M. Quételet also, in his fine treatise on periodic phenomena, handled those topics with ability. The latter *savant* very correctly said: "Astronomy, and particularly the observation of the two great luminaries that strike our gaze the most, may be considered as including the origin of all the phenomena that deserve to engage our studious attention."

Arago, in his "Popular Astronomy," has also pointed out the beauties of the connection that the observation of cosmic and terrestrial phenomena reveals to us:

"The various phenomena of the starry vault and of meteorology, even when they appear by their fickleness to baffle all the perspicacity of men, at length are seen, after profound study, to be linked together in sublime coördination."

M. Renou, in his memoranda on the periodical return of heavy winters, has grouped together the important facts that seem to prove that the period of the principal meteorological phenomena is associated with the periods of the shooting-stars, the solar spots, and the oscillations of the magnetic needle. These relations, although as yet chiefly based upon conjecture, as M. Renou remarks, must nevertheless be our guide in seeking out the great laws that govern the organization of worlds.

It is, above all, by the knowledge of these laws, by the admiration that they imperatively call for in us, that it becomes possible for us to conceive of the beneficent action of the Creative Power; to rise to the idea of Infinite Wisdom, and to taste the ineffable peace of that religious feeling which Leibnitz expressed so well when he said, "It is no trivial thing to be content with God and the universe."

NOTES.

INSTRUMENTS OF OBSERVATION.

The Barometer.—The Thermometer.—The Hygrometer.—The Pluviometer, or Udometer.

THE BAROMETER.

An upright tube of glass, of about 85 centimetres (3⅓ inches) in length, filled with mercury, and standing in a cistern, or basin, also full of the same metal, constitutes a barometer. The atmospheric pressure is measured by the difference of levels established between the tube and the receptacle. Various processes, more or less exact, have been employed to determine this difference.

When no very great precision is required, a large receptacle is used, and no attention is paid to the variations in the level of the mercury that it contains. Sometimes it is considered sufficient to make the scale movable, so as to bring the zero of its subdivisions to the exterior level. In the *siphon* barometer, the tube curved near the foot forms two unequal limbs, the larger of which is closed and the other open. It requires two observations.

Fortin's barometer, by which it is possible to take more accurate observations, has the special advantage of being very portable, but it is dear. It is distinguished from the rest by the circumstance that the level of the mercury in the receptacle can always be adjusted with much precision to the zero of the fixed scale. When the observation is carefully made, the height can be attained within the twentieth part of a millimetre.

Taking the precaution to compare it from time to time with a mercury barometer, the *aneroid* barometer may be employed in meteorological observations. It is composed of a flexible brass tube, and is bent over in a ring that nearly closes. A vacuum is made beforehand, and, when the atmospheric pressure increases or diminishes, the ring closes or opens, and this movement communicates itself to a needle that marks the pressure on an index.

THE THERMOMETER.

The mercury thermometer is usually employed in the observatories, and alcohol does not become necessary except in regions where the cold congeals the metal. The liquid, the dilation of which is to be observed, is enclosed in a capillary glass tube, soldered to a cylindrical or spherical reservoir of the same material. The scale is graduated on the tube itself, or upon a ruled register running parallel to it, the former arrangement being the best. The temperature of melting ice has been taken as the zero of this scale, and for the second fixed point, represented by one hundred degrees, the boiling temperature of distilled water in a metallic receptacle, the atmospheric pressure being $0^m.75$.

In order to ascertain the lowest temperature at night and the highest by day, special instruments are substituted for ordinary thermometers. Rutherford's thermometer, *a minima*, is the simplest. Placed horizontally, or very

INSTRUMENTS OF OBSERVATION. 321

slightly inclined to the side opposite the reservoir, it contains alcohol and an index formed by a small enamelled cylinder. When the liquid contracts, this body is carried with it, by an adhesive effect, up to the point that corresponds with the maximum of contraction. The temperature then rising, the alcohol dilates and passes between the inner surface of the tube and the index, without displacing the later.

The thermometer, *a maxima*, of the same inventor, is also arranged with mercury, and encloses a cylindrical index of iron. The instrument being placed horizontally, and the fluid dilating, the cylinder is pushed before it. It remains in its place when the fluid contracts, because there is no adhesion between mercury and iron. A magnet is employed to reëstablish contact.

The commission of the Scientific Association recommends the thermometer, *a maxima*, of Messrs. Negretti and Zambra, London opticians. It is a mercury thermometer, the stem of which is choked near the reservoir by a point of glass which is soldered to it inside. The mercury passes this obstacle during the increase of temperature; but when it is descending, the thermometer being horizontal, the column of mercury is separated at the obstructed point, and remains in its place. When the observation has been made, it is sufficient to set the instrument upright again and give it a slight shake, in order to make the mercury fall back into the reservoir.

THE HYGROMETER.

When we speak of the hygrometric condition of the atmosphere, we mean the relation between the actual quantity of watery vapor that it contains, and the quantity that it would contain were it saturated, the temperature being the same in both cases. In order to get at this relation, instruments termed *hygrometers* are used. They are constructed in accordance with the property that bodies have of becoming elongated by moisture and contracted by dryness. Another mode of observing humidity is by the *psychrometer*, which consists in simultaneously watching two thermometers, the one dry and the other with its reservoir kept constantly wet.

Saussure's hygrometer is formed of a hair previously freed of grease. Its variations of length are communicated to a needle moving on a marked dial. Zero is fixed at the point where the needle stops when the air is completely dry, and one hundred degrees at the point it touches when the air is saturated with watery vapor. The indications of this instrument are not proportional to the hygrometric condition of the air. In order to obtain the latter, the tables prepared by Gay-Lussac must be used.

In the psychrometer method, the evaporation that takes place on the wet reservoir causes a decrease of temperature, from which, by means of a simple calculation, may be deduced the elastic force of the vapor, and, consequently, the degree of moisture existing in the air.

THE PLUVIOMETER, OR UDOMETER.

The pluviometer, or udometer, is an instrument that serves to measure the quantity of rain that falls during a given time in a given place. Different forms might be described, but one of the most simple is represented in the

INSTRUMENTS OF OBSERVATION. 323

Magasin Pittoresque, vol. xxiv., 1856, p. 192. Considerable improvements were proposed some years ago by M. Hervé-Mangon. The pluviometer of the marine depot, of which we give an illustration, is composed of a double reservoir of tin, with inclined planes, movable upon a central axis, to serve as an overfall. The rain-water being received in a wide funnel, the surface of which is determined according to each apparatus, passes by a conduit into a second reservoir A, above the receptacle B. The water issues from it by a small orifice, and falls upon one of the inclined planes of the receptacle. When a certain amount

PLUVIOMETER.

has flowed off, according to the condition of the apparatus, the receptacle tips back, strikes against a copper stem C C, and the water runs off into a lateral reservoir D D.

This tipping or oscillating movement recurs thus every

time that a sufficient weight of water has fallen. The principal merit of the apparatus is, that it registers of itself the volume of water received : for this purpose there is joined to the horizontal axis E a needle F, the extremity of which plunges into G, a small tank of mercury, every time that the oscillating movement takes place.

During this very brief period an electric current is established : it is produced by two wires, H and K, one of which, K, communicates with L, the foot of the tank, and the other with the mercury G. By means of a special piece of mechanism, the current itself marks a point, each time that the tipping occurs, upon a roll of paper that passes on with a uniform motion. A glance at the sheet will then let us know how much water fell at any given time in the day.

THE END.

D. APPLETON & CO.'S PUBLICATIONS.

NOW READY.

THE MILITARY HISTORY OF
ULYSSES S. GRANT,

From April, 1861, to April, 1865.

By ADAM BADEAU,

Colonel, and Aide-de-Camp to the General-in-Chief, Brevet Brigadier-General U. S. Army.

Volume I. With Portrait and numerous Maps. pp. 580. Price, $4.

FROM THE PREFACE.

"The fact that I became a member of General Grant's personal staff, before he assumed command of the armies of the United States, and that I have since remained with him, is the voucher that I offer for the correctness of this history. I have not meant to state one fact, unless it came under my own personal observation, or has been told me by the General of the Army, or one of his important officers, or unless I know it from official papers. When I deviate from this rule, I make the deviation known.

"The correspondence, telegraphic and written, of the headquarters of the armies, is accessible to me. I have also been allowed to examine all papers under the control of the War Department; and, as many of the rebel archives are now in the possession of the Government, I have seen the original reports made by the rebel generals, of every battle but two, which I have attempted to describe. Those two are Corinth and Iuka, at neither of which General Grant was present in person. The original rebel field returns have also been closely examined by me. No statement of rebel movements or strength is made in this volume, unless taken from these sources; or, if otherwise, the source is named.

"Generals Sherman, Sheridan, Ord, and Wilson, and the officers of General Grant's staff, as well as Admiral Porter, have afforded me much valuable information, and given me all the assistance in their power, that I have desired. The Honorable Edwin M. Stanton has also furnished me with information which I could not otherwise have obtained.

"The present volume brings my narrative down to the period when General Grant was made Lieutenant-General, and assumed command of all the national armies. It refers to scenes and events, many of which I did not personally witness, as I first reported to him, in person, in February, 1864. His private as well as official correspondence, and daily conversation for years with himself and the officers who accompanied him in his earlier campaigns, are my principal authority. I have his permission now to make known whatever I have learned from these various sources.

"My opinions, however, have not been submitted to General Grant. For them I alone am responsible. But, those opinions are based exclusively on the facts presented to the reader, and, unless supported by the evidence I offer, must fall to the ground."

D. APPLETON & CO., Publishers,

90, 92 & 94 Grand Street, New York.

Novel Scholastic Method for the Colloquial Acquisition of Foreign Languages.

In course of publication, in 12mo.

THE MASTERY SERIES

FOR

LEARNING LANGUAGES ON NEW PRINCIPLES.

By THOMAS PRENDERGAST,

Author of 'The Mastery of Languages, or the Art of Speaking Foreign Tongues Idiomatically.'

This method offers a solution of the problem, How to obtain facility in speaking foreign languages grammatically, without using THE GRAMMAR in the first stage. It adopts and systematizes that process by which many couriers and explorers have become expert practical linguists.

JUST PUBLISHED.

HANDBOOK TO THE MASTERY SERIES; being an Introductory Treatise. Price, 50 cents.

THE MASTERY SERIES, GERMAN. Price, 50 cents.

THE MASTERY SERIES, FRENCH. Price, 50 cents.

To be followed shortly by

THE MASTERY SERIES, SPANISH. Price, 50 cents.

THE MASTERY SERIES, HEBREW. Price, 50 cents.

"We know that there are some who have given Mr. Prendergast's plan a trial, and discovered that in a very few weeks its results had surpassed all their anticipations."—*The Record.*

"The Mastery System gives, in our opinion, all the advantages of Ollendorff's, and is free from its defects.... To gain a thorough command of the common phrases which the majority use exclusively and all men chiefly, is the goal at which the mastery system aims, and we think that goal can be reached by its means more easily and in a shorter time than by any method yet made known."—*Norfolk News.*

"Mr. Prendergast's scheme has the merit of simplicity, being nothing more nor less than a deduction from the natural method pursued by children, aided by the reason or intelligence which children do not possess, but which belongs to adults."—*Greenock Advertiser.*

".... En un mot, c'est le système le plus pratique que la philologie ait produit pour l'enseignement des langues étrangères."—*L'Impartial de Boulogne.*

New York: D. APPLETON & CO.

Works published by D. Appleton & Co.

HEAT,
CONSIDERED AS A MODE OF MOTION,

Being a Course of Twelve Lectures delivered before the Royal Institution of Great Britain.

BY JOHN TYNDALL, F. R. S.,

PROFESSOR OF NATURAL PHILOSOPHY IN THE ROYAL INSTITUTION—AUTHOR OF THE "GLACIERS OF THE ALPS," ETC.

With One Hundred Illustrations. 8vo, 480 pages. Price, $2.00.

From the American Journal of Science.—With all the skill which has made Faraday the master of experimental science in Great Britain, Professor Tyndall enjoys the advantage of a superior general culture, and is thus enabled to set forth his philosophy with all the graces of eloquence and the finish of superior diction. With a simplicity, and absence of technicalities, which render his explanations lucid to unscientific minds, and at the same time a thoroughness and originality by which he instructs the most learned, he unfolds all the modern philosophy of heat. His work takes rank at once as a classic upon the subject.

New York Times.—Professor Tyndall's course of lectures on heat is one of the most beautiful illustrations of a mode of handling scientific subjects, which is comparatively new, and which promises the best results, both to science and to literature generally; we mean the treatment of subjects at once *profound* and *popular*. The title of Professor Tyndall's work indicates the theory of heat held by him, and indeed the only one now held by scientific men—*it is a mode of motion.*

Boston Journal.—He exhibits the curious and beautiful workings of nature in a most delightful manner. Before the reader particles of water lock themselves or fly asunder with a movement regulated like a dance. They form themselves into liquid flowers with fine serrated petals, or into rosettes of frozen gauze; they bound upward in boiling fountains, or creep slowly onward in stupendous glaciers. Flames burst into music and sing, or cease to sing, as the experimenter pleases, and metals paint themselves upon a screen in dazzling hues as the painter touches his canvas.

New York Tribune.—The most original and important contribution that has yet been made to the theory and literature of thermotics.

Scientific American.—The work is written in a charming style, and is the most valuable contribution to scientific literature that has been published in many years. It is the most popular exposition of the dynamical theory of heat that has yet appeared. The old material theory of heat may be said to be defunct.

Louisville Democrat.—This is one of the most delightful scientific works we have ever met. The lectures are so full of life and spirit that we can almost imagine the lecturer before us, and see his brilliant experiments in every stage of their progress. The theory is so carefully and thoroughly explained that no one can fail to understand it. Such books as these create a love for science.

Independent.—Professor Tyndall's expositions and experiments are remarkably thoughtful, ingenious, clear, and convincing; portions of the book have almost the interest of a romance, so startling are the descriptions and elucidations.

THE NEW
AMERICAN CYCLOPÆDIA.

D. APPLETON & CO.,
90, 92 & 94 GRAND ST., NEW YORK.

HAVE NOW READY THE

NEW AMERICAN CYCLOPÆDIA,
A POPULAR DICTIONARY OF GENERAL KNOWLEDGE.

EDITED BY

GEORGE RIPLEY and CHARLES A. DANA,

AIDED BY A

Numerous Select Corps of Writers in all Branches of Science, Art, and Literature,

IN 16 LARGE VOLUMES, 8vo,

750 double-column Pages in each Volume.

From the New York Times.

"It is a work written by Americans for Americans. It proffers them the knowledge they most require, selected and arranged by those who are competent to the task, because they themselves had experienced the want they now endeavor to supply. It is minute on points of general interest, and condensed in those of more partial application. Its information is the latest extant, and in advance of any other book of reference in the world. The best talent in the country has been engaged in its production."

PRICE OF THE WORK:

In Extra Cloth, per vol., ... $5 00
In Library Leather, per vol., ...6 00
In Half Turkey Morocco, black, per vol.,......................6 50
In Half Russia, extra gilt, per vol.,............................7 50
In Full Morocco, antique, gilt edges, per vol.,............. ..9 00
In Full Russia,...9 00

The price of the work will, for the present, remain as above, but if there shall be any great advance in paper and material the price must be increased. To prevent disappointment, orders should be at once forwarded to the publishers or to the agents of the work in different parts of the country.

To those who have not already Subscribed for the Work.

Many persons have omitted to subscribe for the Work during its progress through the Press, owing to an unwillingness to subscribe for an incomplete work. They may now obtain complete sets in any of the above Styles.

D. APPLETON & CO., Publishers,
90, 92 & 94 GRAND STREET, NEW YORK.

www.ingramcontent.com/pod-product-compliance
Lightning Source LLC
Chambersburg PA
CBHW020321240426
43673CB00039B/879